"*The Pastor as Leader* recovers the greatest nee̶ the pastor as a man of God who leads throu̶ ambassador. Every page is convicting, and no̶ in prayer, 'O Lord, raise up a generation of men o̶ Spirit and leading from their knees, faithfully preach your word.'"

    Alfred J. Poirier, Professor of Pastoral Theology, Westminster Theological Seminary; author, *The Peacemaking Pastor*

"Good pastors lead and feed—all week long and especially in the pulpit. These two central tasks go together. In his church, Christ means for the rulers to teach and the teachers to rule. Separating one from the other would harm them both. By connecting principles and practices, John Currie helps preacher-leaders realize the ancient, enduring vision. I encourage not only individuals but leadership teams to read this book."

    David Mathis, Senior Teacher and Executive Editor, desiringGod.org; Pastor, Cities Church, Saint Paul, Minnesota; author, *Habits of Grace*

"*The Pastor as Leader* is clear, deeply scriptural, and cogently written. While it reflects the best of the Reformed tradition and its pastoral riches, it is remarkably relevant for all pastors, regardless of denominational tradition or theological connection. This is because John Currie's commitment to and exposition of the Scriptures engage the heart and mind of one called to serve Christ in ministry. This book will inspire both pastoral students and pastors who have served in ministry for many years. I highly recommend it."

    Peter A. Lillback, President, Westminster Theological Seminary

"This book fills a void in the pastoral-leadership literature and has quickly become one of my favorite books on the pastorate. It is filled with robust biblical exegesis, sound theology, affection for Christ, and helpful real-life application. Currie's experience and expertise as a pastor and mentor to pastors shows on every page. Come sit at the feet of this pastor of pastors to be refreshed and renewed in ministry."

    Jason Helopoulos, Senior Pastor, University Reformed Church, East Lansing, Michigan; author, *The New Pastor's Handbook* and *Covenantal Baptism*

"Often when pastors think about leadership in the church, they fail to take into account the strategic place of preaching. With biblical and theological depth, John Currie describes the many facets necessary for the man of God, in the power of God, to effectively lead the flock of God through the ministry of the word of God. This is a book that preachers and aspiring preachers need to read and digest."

Timothy Z. Witmer, author, *The Shepherd Leader*; Professor Emeritus of Practical Theology, Westminster Theological Seminary

"Rather than relying on the latest secular leadership strategies, Currie has written a book that is rich in biblical exposition, careful in the application of theological categories, and informed by noteworthy pastors and theologians throughout the church's history. According to Currie, leadership is an expression of a biblical ecclesiology, requiring clear convictions concerning the church's mission, the purpose of preaching, and an appreciation of the varied gifts the ascended and reigning Christ has distributed within his church. Throughout this book, you will find encouragement to lead, starting with your preaching, with greater conviction and clarity."

Rob Edwards, Associate Professor of Pastoral Theology and Dean of Students, Westminster Theological Seminary

"A pastor is a leader. But where will he lead those who follow him? *The Pastor as Leader* isn't just another book on leadership or preaching but a Scripture-saturated plea to lead God's people by God's word. This refreshing vision of pastoral ministry was helpful and humbling for me. I trust it'll serve you as well."

J. Garrett Kell, Pastor, Del Ray Baptist Church, Alexandria, Virginia; author, *Pure in Heart*

"What does it mean to be a new covenant minister of the Spirit, a post-Pentecost pastor now that Christ—crucified, resurrected, and ascended—is head over all things to and for the church? With sound handling of Scripture, enriched by his own experience as a seasoned pastor, John Currie explores the answer as he makes the compelling case that the pastor's calling as a leader takes place primarily in the pulpit."

Richard B. Gaffin Jr., Professor Emeritus of Biblical and Systematic Theology, Westminster Theological Seminary

The Pastor as Leader

The Pastor as Leader

Principles and Practices for Connecting
Preaching and Leadership

John Currie

Foreword by Sinclair B. Ferguson

:: CROSSWAY®

WHEATON, ILLINOIS

Library of Congress Cataloging-in-Publication Data

Names: Currie, John, 1967– author.
Title: The pastor as leader : principles and practices for connecting preaching and leadership / John Currie.
Description: Wheaton, Illinois : Crossway, 2024. | Includes bibliographical references and index.
Identifiers: LCCN 2023026808 (print) | LCCN 2023026809 (ebook) | ISBN 9781433590153 (trade paperback) | ISBN 9781433590160 (pdf) | ISBN 9781433590184 (epub)
Subjects: LCSH: Clergy. | Christian leadership. | Leadership.
Classification: LCC BV659 .C76 2024 (print) | LCC BV659 (ebook) | DDC 253—dc23/eng/20231004
LC record available at https://lccn.loc.gov/2023026808
LC ebook record available at https://lccn.loc.gov/2023026809

Crossway is a publishing ministry of Good News Publishers.

VP   33   32   31   30   29   28   27   26   25   24
15   14   13   12   11   10   9   8   7   6   5   4   3   2   1

In memoriam
Harry L. Reeder III
man of God

Contents

Foreword

SINCE CONFESSION IS SAID to be good for the soul, I should begin with one: John Currie has been both a friend and an encourager to me for many years. I have long appreciated him as a person and admired the quality of his preaching and the fruitfulness of his pastoral ministry in the congregations he has served. He has a spirit that colleagues, students, and pastors alike respond to, graciously combining considerable personal gifts with a deep and genuine appreciation for the gifts of others. In addition to this, I am also grateful for the special kinds of sacrifice he and his wife, Rhonda, have made to enable him to serve as a professor at Westminster Theological Seminary in Philadelphia, where he invests himself wholeheartedly in preparing others for pastoral ministry. For while seminary teaching is truly a great work, it is a very specific kind of ministry, and for someone who loves the regular, multifaceted life of ministry to a particular church family, it can sometimes feel like a demotion!

In light of this level of affection for the author, readers will understand my necessary element of restraint in commending these pages. But I do commend them enthusiastically, for several reasons. Books on the preaching ministry have become increasingly numerous in recent years. This one, however, has several features that make it distinct. They are almost immediately obvious; but perhaps the most obvious is that—unlike many other contemporary works on ministry and leadership—this one is not driven by the question *What works?*

A friend who pastored a megachurch once told me of a small, select, and by-invitation-only gathering of megachurch pastors to which he had been invited. At the first meeting the men sat round a large table and "the question" was posed for each to answer in turn: "What's *working* in your church?" My friend told me he was very tempted to answer with the single but, alas, unexpected word—"Romans"! For if it is not God's word that is "working" as the shaper and driver of a ministry, and of the life of a church family, the auguries for our eternity-long fruitfulness are not very hopeful. Sharing that conviction, the practical wisdom Dr. Currie provides for us here is very clearly derived from the pages of sacred Scripture and its sacred theology. We can be grateful that his students are in the safe hands of someone for whom Paul's words about both the origin of Scripture ("breathed out by God") and its usefulness ("for teaching, for reproof, for correction, and for training in righteousness, that the man of God may be complete, equipped for every good work"—2 Tim. 3:16–17) underpin his own vision for ministry and the foci of his teaching.

Over the long haul, ministry that builds with materials that will last for eternity cannot afford to be shaped by the latest fad. Fad-driven ministry tends to create doctrinal light-headedness rather than lasting substance. So (to paraphrase some words the great John Owen used to introduce one of his own works) "if you have picked up this book looking for a quick fix, farewell! You have had your entertainment!" These pages demand that you put on your thinking cap. This is a book for long-haul ministry. Its wisdom is based on the principle that the extent to which our minds are soaked in, and our lives shaped by, Scripture will determine the quality of our ministry. Sir Francis Bacon's famous words are applicable here: "Some books are to be tasted, others to be swallowed, and some few to be chewed and digested." *The Pastor as Leader* belongs to this last category, and there will be no other way to absorb and benefit from it than by chewing on what Currie writes and slowly and carefully digesting it. This is practical *theology* as well as theology that is *practical*.

Different readers will come to these pages from different contexts of ministry, needing or looking for different kinds of help, whether instruction, challenge, encouragement, or stimulation. All of these can be found here. But whatever our specific reasons for placing ourselves under Professor Currie's tutelage, he strikes notes that should refresh and benefit us all. One is the way in which he sees the organic relationship between leadership and preaching; others are his emphases on union with Christ, on prayer, and on the ministry of the Spirit.

John Currie has mined deeply in Scripture, as will be obvious from the way in which, on some pages, biblical references seem to be as numerous as punctuation marks. He has also dug deeply in the quarry of the best exponents of pastoral theology, both in theory and in practice, and in doing so reminds us that gold and precious stones are still to be found in the literature to which today's pastors are privileged heirs.

The Pastor as Leader is not a quick read, although it is worth reading through once quickly in order to be prepared to read it again slowly, page by page, reflecting on the helpful and probing questions with which each chapter ends. I very much hope that as you read, you will find that John Currie is a pastor's Barnabas, and that he will be as much of a son of encouragement to you as he has been to me.

Sinclair B. Ferguson

Acknowledgments

I AM GRATEFUL, beyond words, to God, who has allowed me to serve as a pastor and a professor for pastors. The stewardship of the word in both capacities is a sacred trust. That this has now been extended to offering a book in the service of pastors is a privilege of indescribable grace.

In his providence God has used many to teach, mentor, and support me in order to bring this book to its readers. I am thankful for the faculty who taught me at Westminster Theological Seminary, some of whom have become my colleagues, for training me in the sufficiency of Scripture and the centrality of Christ for pastoral leadership and all of life. I am particularly indebted to Richard B. Gaffin Jr., my teacher and exemplar, who gave of his time to review this manuscript and provide his insights and opinions on its biblical and theological argumentation. Any weaknesses that remain in this regard are, of course, my own. Harry Reeder, my friend and mentor to whose memory this book is dedicated, was taken into the presence of the Lord before he had opportunity to review it, but his instruction, inspiration, and influence are stamped throughout its pages, as well as my life and ministry.

I would be remiss, in a book such as this, if I did not express my thanks to the many elders and pastors with whom I have had the privilege of serving over the years. Their patience, encouragement, and iron-sharpening partnership have allowed the theory in these pages to be tried, tested, and improved in the context of pastoral ministry, I trust, to the edification of the congregations we have served together.

Thanks are also due to the trustees and administration of Westminster for providing me with a study leave to complete this book, and especially to Dr. and Mrs. Gregory Poland for their generous provision of the research grant to support the study leave in which this book was written.

I thank Crossway for believing this book was worthy of their investment, for their excellence of execution in bringing it to publication, and for providing the expert editorial skill of Thom Notaro. Uriah Renzetti also invested a great deal of time and skill in editing the manuscript prior to its submission, for which his former professor is deeply grateful.

Finally, I cannot adequately express my gratitude for and to "the redhead," my wife, Rhonda. How does one say thank you in a few short lines for a lifetime of selfless love, humble and courageous wisdom, and unwavering support through the valleys and victories in service of Christ's cause? The Lord has used you, more than anyone else on earth, and your trust in Christ, commitment to his word, integrity of life, and timely counsel to inspire and hold me accountable to be God's man for God's glory. I and this book would not be here without you.

All Scripture is breathed out by God and profitable for teaching, for reproof, for correction, and for training in righteousness, that the man of God may be complete, equipped for every good work. . . . Preach the word.

2 TIMOTHY 3:16–17; 4:2

The pastor by definition is a shepherd, the undershepherd of the flock of God. His primary task is to feed the flock by leading them to green pastures.

WILLIAM STILL

Introduction

A Vision for Connecting Preaching and Leadership

PREACHING IS LEADERSHIP in Christ's cause. This book has been written to train pastors who will lead the church on its mission in the next generation to connect their preaching with leadership. I have become convinced, through the study and practice of pastoral ministry for over thirty years in a variety of denominational contexts, that an unbiblical divorce often occurs between the pastoral priorities of preaching and leadership more generally. When this happens, the church suffers from either stagnation on its mission or a downgrade in the pulpit. *The Pastor as Leader* seeks to equip pastors to effectively steward their responsibilities as leaders in Christ's cause while being unashamedly committed to preaching as the primary means by which Christ extends his church's mission in the world.

The Problem: An Unnecessary Disconnect

Many pastors feel an irreconcilable disconnect between the priority of preaching and the pressing responsibilities of leadership, and conclude that they must choose between the two. One end of the disconnect was illustrated for me by a pastoral candidate who was asked by a search committee considering recommending him for the leadership of a congregation, "What was the last book you read on leadership?" His answer was "Oh, I would never do something like that!" He assumed that being conversant in the principles and practices of leadership would necessarily compromise his commitment to biblical methods of ministry. The other end can be poignantly illustrated by the well-publicized case of a pastor who had, for many years, been using the sermons of others and passing them off as his own. When exposed, he responded that his church required so much investment from him as a leader that he could not afford the time to study the Scriptures to prepare sermons. Illustrations on each side could be multiplied.

Albert Mohler summarizes the division between what he terms "the Believers" and "the Leaders" this way: The Believers are driven by their beliefs and dedicated to learning, teaching, and defending truth but are not equipped to lead; they "are afraid that thinking too much about it will turn them into mere pragmatists." The Leaders are "masters of change and organizational transformation" who are tired of seeing churches decline and "want to change things for the better" but "lack a center of gravity in truth." Mohler observes that "the evangelical Christian world is increasingly divided" between these groups.[1]

This book addresses this problem where it manifests itself in the pastorate, between "the Preachers" and "the Leaders," because this unnecessary division harms the church and hinders its mission. A congregation needs leadership to be faithful and fruitful in its

---

1 Albert Mohler, *The Conviction to Lead: 25 Principles for Leadership That Matters* (Minneapolis: Bethany, 2012), 20.

Christ-appointed mission, and in Christ's kingdom that leadership must come through his word preached. If a pastor doesn't understand his identity and calling as a leader, that will disable not only his leadership but also his preaching, because he will lack holy zeal to take anyone anywhere with what he says. If he assumes the responsibility to lead without an immovable conviction of the primacy of biblical preaching, he will put the church at risk of being driven by voices other than the chief shepherd's. When the two essential pastoral functions of preaching and leadership become disintegrated from each other, the church suffers from either inertia on its mission or a decline in quality from its pulpit. When leadership is neglected, preaching can devolve into a mere intellectual and informational exercise, which lacks power to transform a congregation. When preaching is deprioritized, God's word becomes functionally subordinated to the authority of leadership trends and techniques, and faithful interpretation is negotiated or manipulated in deference to worldly leadership aspirations.

The unnecessary disconnect between these two essential pastoral responsibilities has multiple causes. One prominent cause is extrabiblical organizational theory undiscerningly imposed upon the church. Pastoral leadership is held captive by pragmatism.[2] The values and methods marketed as successful for organizations outside of the church are uncritically appropriated by leaders of the church in the pursuit of a ministry model that "works," as defined by the culture. The preacher assumes

---

2 *Pragmatism* as a philosophy, which says "the ends justify the means," must be carefully distinguished from the ability to be *practical* (put right precepts and principles into practice). The latter, as we shall see, is integral to pastoral leadership.

the role of ecclesiastical CEO, and little of his time is devoted to the earnest study and preparation of God's word as his main service to the church.

A second cause is a particular kind of theologizing about the status quo in the health of a church and its mission. A congregation's stagnation (or regress) in biblical indicators of ministry maturity is rationalized to insulate the pastor's or the congregation's comfort zone. In this system, leaders can repeat misapplications of doctrine to mask their loss of zeal for the extension of Christ's kingdom. The observable atrophy of Christ's body, the church, does not burden the preacher's heart or influence the disciplines of his stewardship, since he aspires to nothing more than the transfer of accurate textual and doctrinal information week to week.

A third cause is the sinful and harmful behavior by once seemingly effective preacher-leaders. Confusion and deep distrust can result from preachers' abuse of the authority that comes with leadership, and this erodes confidence that those who fill pulpits can be trusted with hearts, lives, and families. For some of God's people, the corruption of a trusted pastor has confirmed their fear that leadership is inherently "toxic," especially if that leadership wields God's word as its primary instrument. Disillusioned members are tempted to insulate themselves, spiritually and emotionally, from allowing the stewards of God's word to exercise the leadership influence and carry out the mission for which God has ordained them.

Whatever the reasons, the disconnect between preaching and leadership is both biblically unnecessary and unhealthy for the mission of Christ's church.

The Solution: A Biblical Connection

This book will present what I believe is a biblical and therefore better model: pastoral leadership by appointment of Christ and in union with Christ that prioritizes preaching the word of Christ on the mission of Christ. There is a better way to lead Christ's church on its mission than atheological, pragmatic adoption of corporate culture; self-preserving complacency regarding the status quo; or self-serving, unloving lording over God's people. That better way is pastoral leadership stewarded under Christ's appointment, conformed to Christ's character, exemplifying and implementing Christ's wisdom as preached from Christ's word. As we will see, because Christ leads his kingdom through his word preached, *preaching is leadership* and preachers are leaders in Christ's cause. The question the gospel preacher must answer is not whether he will be a leader but how he will steward the leadership entrusted to him. The chapters that follow aim to equip pastors to steward this calling intentionally, earnestly, and competently.

What to Expect

The Pastor as Leader is an apologetic for pastoral leadership through preaching. It presents biblical and theological arguments to persuade pastors that on Christ's mission they are called *to lead* and that they must lead *as preachers*. For this reason, the book is not primarily a how-to manual. Though it is practical and intentionally moves from principles to practices (most chapters include suggested steps for application), the goal is to show pastors *why* they must engage in leadership and *how* that engagement connects with their preaching. This does not mean multiplying leadership tasks that compete for time with the preacher's stewardship of Scripture. It means, on Christ's mission, that preaching *is* leadership, and the best leadership practices should flow organically from a faithful stewardship of the Scriptures. The goal is to equip preachers to lead as a matter of conviction and from a sense of calling, rather than to bear leadership as a burden born of mere expediency, an adjunct to true ministry—or a substitute for it.

Given this book's brevity, I try to be concise with biblical and theological arguments and to provide further explanation or readings in the notes, where needed. I trust that readers will understand that, given the focus of the book, I have not addressed every issue (some important) that might be relevant to the arguments made.

How to Get There

The first half of the book (chaps. 1–5) will address principles of pastoral leadership that are essential to the practices addressed in the second half (chaps. 6–10). Each chapter seeks to provide encouraging examples of pastoral leadership and succinct but substantive biblical foundations for the practical takeaways that follow. Because Christ leads his kingdom through his word preached, chapters 7–10 are dedicated to demonstrating and defending the functional priority of preaching (i.e., the Christ-centered exposition of the Scriptures) in core elements of pastoral leadership. But this is not another book on Christ-centered hermeneutics and homiletics. The focus here will be on how such preaching functions to lead Christ's church into his purposes. Nor will I directly address some of the vital leadership functions fulfilled by pastors, such as the private ministry of the word in pastoral care and counseling. This book proceeds from the conviction that the pastor's leadership through preaching will fuel and form other necessary expressions of his leadership for the church. In other words, there is a lot of other vital ministry downstream from preaching. In fact, it is *all* downstream from preaching.

Early on I'll seek to establish that *man of God* is an important motif for understanding the pastor's role in leading God's people into God's purpose by preaching God's word. Not only was *man of God* used by Paul, at the end of his apostolic ministry, to orient Timothy to his identity and duty in pastoral leadership at Ephesus, but it reached back to Moses, the prophet God sent to lead his people out of slavery and into his service. In the Scriptures a man of God was God's man sent to proclaim God's word to lead God's people into God's purposes. He was a *preacher-leader*! However, this focus on the preacher as a leader does not imply a single-elder model of church leadership. A pastor is not an Old Testament prophet or a New Testament apostle, and he has not been entrusted with the unique, singular authority of either. The conviction throughout this book is that pastors steward their particular leadership functions as one among a plurality of elders, who together govern and lead Christ's church. The principles and practices advocated in these chapters are all designed to be practiced in a context where the pastor serves as one *on par with* other elders of the church.[3]

---

3 Consider John Murray's comments in his exposition of Rom. 12:8, "the one who leads, with zeal," where he disabuses the interpretation that singular reference to leadership suggests a single elder model. Murray writes: "It would be absurd to suppose that there is any allusion here to government as exercised by one man. The other passages imply a plurality of elders (*cf.* also Acts 15:2, 4, 6, 22, 23; 16:4; 20:17, 28; Titus 1:5; Heb. 13:7, 17). The apostle uses the singular in this case after the pattern followed in the other four instances without any reference to the number of those who might possess and exercise the several gifts. Hence no support could be derived from this text for the idea of one man as president in the government of the church nor of one man

Nonetheless, because our focus will be on the pastor as leader, I will not directly address leadership roles exercised by others in the church or the leadership exercised by Christians in spheres beyond the church. These are high callings for Christ's people and are worthy of entire books dedicated to them. My hope is that this book will be useful to those who lead the church alongside their pastor or who lead for Christ's sake in other spheres. As I have said and we shall further see, all leadership in Christ's cause flows downstream from his word preached. When pastoral leadership is not stewarded competently (or not done at all), other leaders in kingdom stewardship carry the added burden of swimming upstream. When preachers are equipped to lead competently, the Christians they serve will be encouraged and better equipped for leadership in their own God-appointed callings.

The Pastor as Leader is written to equip pastors in their God-given identity as preacher-leaders with some best practices for leading the church through preaching in Christ's mission. If you have a heart for that mission, and you want to refresh and retool for the role Christ has entrusted to you in his church, I invite you to read on. We'll start by regaining clarity of vision for the mission on which Christ has sent us.

---

as chief over those who rule." And "every infraction upon or neglect of government directly prejudices the witness to the truth of which the church is the pillar." John Murray, *The Epistle to the Romans* (Glenside, PA: Westminster Seminary Press, 2022), 449. Readers should keep Murray's conviction in mind as they read the rest of this book and attempt to apply its principles and practices in their ecclesiastical contexts.

PART 1

———————

PRINCIPLES

*All authority in heaven and on earth has been
given to me. Go therefore and make disciples.*

MATTHEW 28:18–19

*Our plans and efforts for promoting this object ought . . . to
be large, liberal, and ever expanding. . . . When we direct our
attention to the spread of the Gospel, our views, our prayers,
our efforts are all too stinted and narrow. We scarcely ever
lift our eyes to the real grandeur and claims of the enterprise
in which we profess to be engaged. . . . We are too apt to be
satisfied with small and occasional contributions of service
to this greatest of all causes instead of devoting to it hearts
truly enlarged; instead of desiring great things; expecting
great things; praying for great things; and nurturing in our
spirits that holy elevation of sentiment and affection, which
embraces in its desires and prayers the entire kingdom of God.*

SAMUEL MILLER

1

The Mission of a Man of God

The Greatest of All Causes

ALEXANDER DUFF served as a missionary to India from the Church of Scotland. When he returned on furlough in 1836, he saw that the theological winds of modernism were beginning to drive the church, bringing an apathy toward the missionary task Christ committed to his church. So, Duff preached! In 1836 he preached for two hours before the General Assembly, and in 1839 he traveled from one congregation to another, preaching a sermon that Hughes Oliphant Old identifies as "one of the most significant sermons ever preached."[1] The sermon was taken from Psalm 67 and titled "Missions the Chief End of the Christian Church." Duff applied the gospel-promising logic of the psalm to the church's commitment to missions, saying, "When a Church

1 Hughes Oliphant Old, *The Reading and Preaching of the Scriptures in the Worship of the Christian Church*, vol. 6, *The Modern Age* (Grand Rapids, MI: Eerdmans, 2007), 679.

ceases to be evangelistic, it must cease to be evangelical; and when it ceases to be evangelical, it must cease to exist as a true Church of God, however primitive or apostolic it may be in its outward form and constitution!"[2] He concluded with a sobering historical analysis:

> What is the whole history of the Christian church but one perpetual proof and illustration of the grand position,—that an evangelistic or missionary Church is a spiritually flourishing Church, and, that a church which drops the evangelistic or missionary character, speedily lapses into superannuation [obsolescence] and decay![3]

Duff connected the church's commitment to its Christ-entrusted mission with its ability to remain faithful to its apostolic foundations and spiritually vital. He saw that no matter how right its outward forms might be, when a church loses its sense of mission (in that case, through the sepsis of liberalism), it atrophies and eventually fails to be what Christ commissioned it to be in the world. So, he preached.

This book grows out of the conviction that Christ leads his church through his word preached; therefore, preaching is leadership in Christ's cause. And if the church is to be led on its Christ-

---

2 Alexander Duff, *Missions the Chief End of the Christian Church* (London: Forgotten Books, 2015), 12. For a similar sentiment, see Richard B. Gaffin Jr., "The Holy Spirit," *Westminster Theological Journal* 43, no. 1 (1980): 73, where Gaffin writes, "It cannot be stressed too emphatically, then, that the Spirit of Pentecost is the Spirit of *mission* . . . ; where the church is no longer a witnessing church, whether in the immediate, local or world-wide context, it has lost contact with its Pentecostal roots" (emphasis original).

3 Duff, *Missions The Chief End*, 30.

commissioned mission, pastors must be clear about that mission, committed to it, and preach in a way that leads God's people into God's purposes for them. Pastors must, as J. W. Alexander put it, be "yielded up to the cause of the Lord Jesus, in the spirit of sacrifice, with no limitation or evasion of his bonds."[4] Otherwise, preaching loses its leadership impetus, and the goal of preaching, Sunday after Sunday, can become merely to transmit accurate information or simply "not get it wrong" (the *minimum* threshold for faithful stewardship, cf. 2 Tim. 2:15). When weary, war-torn pastors stop longing and laboring to see the message they preach mature the saints in God's purposes for them and to see sinners won by God's grace, preaching becomes "all too stinted and narrow" and loses its sense of place and purpose in God's glorious plan. Heralds of the greatest message in all the world must steward their task with hearts and eyes fixed on the greatest cause in all of history, extending the redeeming righteous rule of God, through Christ their King, to the hearts and lives of multitudes of disciples, to the end of the earth until the end of the age.

Christ the King leads his church on his mission through his word preached. This is the foundation for the vital connection between preaching and leadership. In chapter 7 we'll see that Christ gave preaching pride of place during his earthly ministry and now still does from heaven. In this chapter we'll see that he did that as *the leader* of God's people on mission to establish God's rule in their hearts and lives. A survey of

---

4 J. W. Alexander, "Considerations on Foreign Missions Addressed to Candidates for the Holy Ministry," in *Princeton and the Work of the Christian Ministry: A Collection of Addresses, Essays, and Articles by Faculty and Friends of Princeton Theological Seminary*, ed. James M. Garretson, 2 vols. (Carlisle, PA: Banner of Truth, 2012), 2:67.

Luke's introduction to Jesus and his mission-defining sermon in Nazareth (Luke 4:16–27) will show us that Christ prioritized preaching as Christ *the King, the leader* God sent to establish his promised kingdom.

The Leader and His Mission

From the beginning of his Gospel, Luke is concerned to convince his readers that Jesus is the promised messianic King (1:4). Luke's account of Jesus's birth emphasizes that he was descended from "the house of David" (1:27) and was to be given "the throne of his father David," from which he was to "reign" over a "kingdom" that will have no end (1:32–33). Jesus was also revealed to be the holy Son of God, because he was conceived by the Holy Spirit as the "power of the Most High" (1:35). His royal identity is then emphasized once again in Zechariah's hymn of praise (1:69–70) and the place of Jesus's birth, "in the city of David" (2:11). Luke then recounts Jesus's baptism, when—according to his human nature—he was anointed with the Holy Spirit for his public ministry as the Christ, and the heavenly voice declared him to be God's beloved and well-pleasing Son (3:22). Jesus's genealogy then identifies him as the "son of Joseph" (3:30), a "son of David" (3:31), descended from Adam as "the son of God" (3:38), directly before Jesus's temptation, which has as its central issue Jesus's identity as *the Son of God* (4:3, 9) and the attainment of a kingdom and authority (4:5–6).

This background is foundational to our topic because "Son of God" was used by biblical writers not only to refer to Jesus as the second person of the Trinity, in his divine nature as *God the Son* (John 1:1, 18; 3:16; 17:5; Rom. 8:3; Col. 1:15–17, 19; Gal. 4:4;

Phil. 2:6; Heb.1:2–3)[5] but also to identify Jesus from the perspective of his singularly determinative place in redemptive history as the now incarnate Son, in terms of his *messianic office* (Luke 4:3, 9; Acts 9:20, 22; Rom. 1:4; Heb. 1:2, 4).[6] "Son of God" had been used previously of Adam (Luke 3:38), Israel (Hos. 11:1; cf. Matt.

---

5 John Murray emphasized that the priority is put on the divine nature: "The title 'Son of God' is one predicated of our Lord in virtue of his pre-temporal, ontological, intertrinitarian identity and relationship." John Murray, "Jesus the Son of God," in *Collected Works of John Murray*, vol. 4, *Studies in Theology* (Edinburgh: Banner of Truth, 1982), 63. Murray provides copious evidence to the effect that the "intra-divine Sonship is always *prior and basic* in the title 'Son' " (71, emphasis added) and that the "eternal, intra-divine, ontological Sonship is *primary* and *basic* in the title 'Son' as predicated of our Lord." Yet "the title 'Son of God' with its distinctly ontological import occurs in the context in which our Lord's messianic office, commission, prerogative, and functions occupy a prominent place" (73, emphasis added). Geerhardus Vos concurs: "The Messiahship is in Jesus' life *the secondary thing*, not merely in the order of being, but *also in the order of importance*." Geerhardus Vos, *The Self-Disclosure of Jesus: The Modern Debate about the Messianic Consciousness*, ed. Johannes Geerhardus Vos (Phillipsburg, NJ: P&R, 2002), 102 (emphasis added).

6 Brandon Crowe makes the point this way: "The contours of Jesus's sonship are multifaceted, at once communicating Jesus's ontological filial relationship to his Father, announcing Jesus's messiahship . . . , evoking corporate Israel . . . , and recalling Adam's royal-filial sonship." Brandon D. Crowe, *The Last Adam: A Theology of the Obedient Life of Jesus in the Gospels* (Grand Rapids, MI: Baker, 2017), 70. For an extended discussion of these uses of the title *Son of God* and their relationship, see Vos, *The Self-Disclosure of Jesus*, 105–225. Vos provides a survey of the "Biblico-theological" background for the various uses of the title *Son of God*. Among them he identifies "the official or Messianic sense in which *it describes not essential nature but office; as the heir and representative of God the Messiah could bear the title of Son of God* without explicit reflection upon His nature; in this official sense God declared to David that not only his Messianic descendant, but also the earlier kings of his line, would be sons to him." Vos, *The Self-Disclosure of Jesus*, 141–42 (emphasis added). Bavinck also sees theocratic kingship in the Old Testament background: "The theocratic king, embodied especially in David . . . was *a son of God* (2 Sam. 7:14; Pss. 2:6–7; 89:27), *the anointed one par excellence* (Pss. 2:2; 18:50)." Herman Bavinck, *Reformed Dogmatics*, ed. John Bolt, trans. John Vriend, vol. 3, *Sin and Salvation in Christ* (Grand Rapids, MI: Baker, 2006), 244 (emphasis added). For a development of the Davidic, theocratic, and messianic background to the use of the title *son*, especially in Paul, see David B. Garner, "The Gospel of God concerning His Beloved Son: Further Steps on a Well-Traveled Text," *Westminster Theological Journal* 84, no. 2 (2022): 257–79.

2:15), and Israel's Davidic king (2 Sam. 7:14; Pss. 2:6–7; 89:27), not because they were divine but because they were appointed by God to bear his image and to serve as God's royal representatives on earth. These fallen and fallible representatives pointed forward to *the Son*, who would be the perfectly obedient and infallibly wise last-days ruler, the Spirit-anointed Christ (Isa. 9:6; 11:1–5). Precisely because Jesus is uniquely qualified by virtue of his divine nature to fulfill the office, "Son of God" is used of Jesus in this messianic sense in Scripture.[7] Through his narrative of Jesus's birth, baptism, and temptation Luke introduces Jesus as the promised divine and Davidic ruler, who has come to defeat God's and his people's enemies and establish God's promised eternal kingdom, Christ *the King*.[8]

This is important for understanding the connection between preaching and leadership in Christ's cause. When, in Luke 4, Christ delivered his mission-defining sermon in Nazareth (4:16–27) and disclosed his messianic identity (4:17, 21) and method (4:16–30, 43–44), we see him delivering his mandate as the

---

7 Vos writes: "Our Lord's eternal sonship qualifies Him for filling the office of Messiah. This office is such and implies such a relation of close affiliation with God, such an acting as the absolute representative of God, such a profound communion of life and purpose with God, that only a Son in the highest sense can adequately fill the office. Thus the office of Messiahship calls for *a Son*." Vos, *The Self-Disclosure of Jesus*, 190. See also Herman Bavinck, *Reformed Dogmatics*, ed. John Bolt, trans. John Vriend, vol. 2, *God and Creation* (Grand Rapids, MI: Baker, 2004), 275.

8 On the relation of Jesus's baptism to his messianic identity, Richard B. Gaffin Jr. writes: "The voice from heaven declares approval of Jesus in his identity as the Messiah. Since to speak of the Messiah is to speak of his kingdom, this declaration amounts to his kingdom commission. The voice of the Father addressed to the Son affirms the appointment of his Son as the Messiah on behalf of the kingdom." Richard B. Gaffin Jr., *In the Fullness of Time: An Introduction to the Biblical Theology of Acts and Paul* (Wheaton, IL: Crossway, 2022), 82.

King, the promised *leader* of God's people.[9] We also begin to see the grandeur of the mission Christ came to lead through the response, tragic as it was, of the people who heard him (4:22, 28–29) and through Christ's open declaration of the purpose of his preaching (4:43). The congregation in the synagogue pivoted dramatically from astonishment (4:22) to attempted assassination (4:28–29). While Christ announced the good news of the arrival of the age of God's promised blessing for his people (4:19), the Israelite crowd marveled. But when he diagnosed the hardness of their hearts, which would result in their rejection of him (4:23), and used their own Scriptures to show that the favor of the Lord would be received by the Gentiles (4:24–27), they turned on him.

The King's mission and its blessings would be rejected by his own people (Israel) but received by the peoples (Gentiles). Blindness and hardness to the extent of Christ's mission was not only tragic but culpable on the part of God's people because God had revealed his purpose and promise to spread his blessings to all peoples in the Old Testament Scriptures, not least through Abraham (Gen. 12:2–3; cf. 13:3–16; 15:4–6). This promise would extend the recognition of God's rule (kingdom) to the ends of the earth (Pss. 67:1–7; 97:1; Isa. 2:1–3; Dan. 7:14) and be executed by the King (2 Sam. 7:12–16; Pss. 2:7–11; 110:1–7; Isa. 9:2, 6–7; 11:1–16) whom God would send as his servant (Isa. 42:1–4; 52:10; 61:1–2). Christ flatly stated this as the purpose for which

---

9 As Messiah and mediator, Jesus was and is not only King but also Prophet and Priest. While Christ as King receives particular focus in this book, and one or another office comes into view on particular occasions in his ministry, it must be remembered always and throughout this work that "essentially Jesus was at all times and places busy in all three offices simultaneously." Herman Bavinck, *The Wonderful Works of God* (Glenside, PA: Westminster Seminary Press, 2019), 314.

he had been sent and the end toward which he preached (Luke 4:18–19, 21; cf. Mark 1:15). When the people at Capernaum also attempted to keep his blessings for themselves, by keeping him for themselves (Luke 4:42),[10] Christ gave them his mission statement: "I must preach the good news of the kingdom of God to the other towns as well; for I was sent for this purpose" (Luke 4:43).[11] Through his preaching, Christ the King was doing nothing less than announcing and establishing the promised *kingdom of God*.

We should understand what this means for the mission Christ came to lead. The kingdom of God is described more than defined in the New Testament.[12] But its description can be summarized this way:

The promised rule of God, for his glory, through his Son, by his Spirit, which is now established and extending in the hearts and lives of Christ's disciples and is yet to be revealed in the outward-bodily creation at his return and the resurrection at the end of this age.[13]

---

10 See James R. Edwards, *The Gospel according to Luke*, The Pillar New Testament Commentary (Grand Rapids, MI: Eerdmans, 2015), 148.

11 See Darrell L. Bock, *Luke*, vol. 1, *1:1–9:50*, Baker Exegetical Commentary on the New Testament (Grand Rapids, MI: Baker, 1994), 422.

12 Vos writes: "We must not expect to find anywhere in his teaching a definition of the kingdom. Jesus' method of teaching was not the philosophical one of defining a thing, but the popular, parabolic one of describing and illustrating it. Paul, though speaking much less of the kingdom, has come much nearer to defining it than our Lord, cf. Rom. 14:17." Geerhardus Vos, *The Teaching of Jesus concerning the Kingdom of God and the Church*, ed. John H. Kerr, 2nd ed. (New York: American Tract Society, 1903), 81–82.

13 This summary is my own. For a thorough development of the concept of the kingdom of God that is assumed and foundational throughout this book, see Gaffin, *In the Fullness of Time*, 65–117; Hermann Ridderbos, *The Coming of the Kingdom* (Philadelphia:

God is King over all his creation all of the time (Pss. 22:28; 99:1; 103:19; 145:11–13). But he promised through his prophets that a time (an age) would come when his righteous rule would be revealed and received universally and unendingly (1 Chron. 17:14; Isa. 9:7; Dan. 2:44; 4:3; 7:14).[14] The coming of God's rule would mean redemption and renewal for God's people (Isa. 9:1–5; 40:1–2; 51:11; 61:2–7; Joel 2:32–3:1) and retribution and wrath for God's enemies (Pss. 2:5–6, 12; 110:1, 5–6; Isa. 61:2). Jesus's arrival as the Son of God meant that the promised kingdom had *now* come, though its inauguration awaited his death and resurrection, together with his subsequent pouring out of the Spirit, and its consummate realization *still* awaits his return in glory (Luke 16:16; 17:21; 22:16, 18, 29–30; 1 Cor. 15:23–28; Rom. 8:21–23). When Christ preached the good news of the kingdom of God, he was proclaiming that through him and his work of redemption (his representative obedience, substitutionary sacrifice, and life-giving resurrection) this kingdom was *now* present *in* those who would receive him through repentance and faith, but that its revelation in the rest of creation and its final judgment of those who would resist him had *not yet* occurred. Christ the King's mission was to establish (inaugurate) this promised age of

---

Presbyterian and Reformed, 1962), 1–174; and Geerhardus Vos, *The Teaching of Jesus concerning the Kingdom of God and the Church* (Eugene, OR: Wipf and Stock, 1998).

14 "It became possible for our Lord to subsume under the notion of the kingdom the entire complex of blessing and glory which the coming order of things would involve for the people of God, and yet to keep before men's minds the thought that this new world of enjoyment was to be enjoyed as a world of God." Vos, *The Teaching of Jesus* (1903), 24. I am indebted to my colleague Jonathan Gibson in his unpublished lecture "Kingdom through Covenant" for some of the Old Testament background in this section.

God's rule and extend it through his church (Luke 24:46–49) to the hearts and lives of multitudes from all peoples.

The Mission of the King and the Mission of His Church

Why spill ink describing the kingdom in a book on pastoral leadership? Because this is the mission on which Christ has appointed pastors to lead his church. When he issued his "Great Commission," Christ grounded it in the fact that he is the risen King, who has been given "all authority in heaven and on earth" (Matt. 28:18), and the purpose of the commission was to extend his rule in hearts and lives, to make disciples who obey all of Christ's commands (Matt. 28:19). Christ had previously described the mission he would commit to his church as proclaiming the kingdom (Matt. 24:14; Luke 9:2), and his post-resurrection instruction to his apostles about their mission was focused on the kingdom (Acts 1:3, 6–8). When the apostles executed the mission Christ had committed to them, they understood it in terms of the kingdom (Acts 20:25; 28:23, 31).[15] The Great Commission is a kingdom-extending mission to spread the rule of God for his glory through his Son to countless hearts and lives until Christ comes again.[16] This is the mission that must capture the heart of a man of God and compel his leadership.

---

15 See Gaffin, *In the Fullness of Time*, 79–80.

16 R. B. Kuiper described the Great Commission, in light of Christ's rule over the whole universe, as commanding all men to "recognize him as king and observe whatsoever things he has commanded." R. B. Kuiper, *The Glorious Body of Christ* (Carlisle, PA: Banner of Truth, 1966), 198. As Gaffin puts it, in applying the consequences of Pentecost to the mission of the church, the church has been given "responsibility and power to witness to the saving, new creation *lordship of Jesus Christ* over the *whole of life* throughout the entire creation." Gaffin, "The Holy Spirit," 73 (emphasis mine).

We should also be aware that confused or compromised visions of what the kingdom of God is in this age can distract or derail pastors from the mission they have been appointed to lead. Greg Gilbert has pointed out that the kingdom of God is not a category most Christians are conversant in or clear on, and too often it is appropriated by theological liberals in the service of "a certain political agenda having to do with broadened social services or a more robust welfare state."[17] The recent years of chaos and conflict over social and political issues in evangelical and Reformed churches are evidence that we need clarity about what the kingdom of God is and is not. In this age, the kingdom of God and its extension come in the salvation of sinners (in all of its gracious blessings and benefits) rather than the transformation of societies.[18] To be sure, Christ's disciples obey all of his

---

17 Kevin DeYoung and Greg Gilbert, *What Is the Mission of the Church? Making Sense of Social Justice, Shalom, and the Great Commission* (Wheaton, IL: Crossway, 2011), 115. Earlier, Edmund Clowney identified how the liberalizing approach reinterpreted the mission of the church as "the liberation of the oppressed," defined in terms of "the struggle for political justice," and had defined the kingdom and salvation in terms of "the doctrines of Karl Marx, accepted as social science." Edmund P. Clowney, *The Church*, Contours of Christian Theology (Downers Grove, IL: InterVarsity Press, 1995), 156.

18 See Gresham Machen, *Christianity and Liberalism* (1923; repr., Philadelphia: Westminster Seminary Press, 2019), 156–60. Machen distinguished between the liberal and Christian understandings of the kingdom, pointing out that in Christianity the kingdom can be entered only by the "divine means of salvation," which is to be found "at the foot of the cross" (38). For Machen, this was "one of the most obvious lines of cleavage between Christianity and the liberal church" (157). Following Machen, R. B. Kuiper accurately assessed the situation in his generation by writing: "The liberal social gospel does much talking about the kingship of Christ, but it denies so many cardinal truths of the Christian religion that it has forfeited every just claim to Christianity. One of its most fateful errors is the divorcing of the kingship of Christ from his cross. . . . It is a simple fact that no sinner will ever honor Christ as Lord who has not first found Him as Savior." Kuiper, *The Glorious Body of Christ*, 198–99.

commands by loving God and doing *whatever* they do, *wherever* they do it, for his glory in Christ's name in the spheres of society where he has sovereignly placed them (Matt. 22:39; 1 Cor. 10:31; Col. 3:17). This means they obey their King by also loving their neighbors and doing (biblically warranted) good works toward their neighbors as they live with them in the relationships that constitute societies (Matt. 5:16; 22:39; Luke 10:37; Eph. 2:10). But we should not equate the outward bodily *effects* of their good works on the institutions and systems of cultures in this age with the coming of the kingdom of God.[19]

To be clear, the kingdom mission of the church, which a man of God has been set apart and sent to lead, is this: to extend the rule of God for God's glory, by proclaiming Christ in his death and resurrection for sinners from all of Scripture, so that multitudes of disciples are made from all nations, through repentance and faith, who submit all of their lives to the rule of Christ and his commands (Matt. 28:18–20; Luke 24:46–48). It is nothing less than extending the redeeming righteous rule of God, through

19 Because Christ the King lives and rules by his Spirit in the hearts and lives of believers, the kingdom of God has *now* come and is *now* present *in them* and the church into which he formed them (cf. Westminster Confession of Faith 25.2 and chap. 2 of this book). By obeying all that Christ has commanded them in all the spheres in which he has placed them, disciples of Christ serve as witnesses to their King and his kingdom. However, the coming of God's kingdom in the outward-bodily creation (of which the institutions and structures of society and cultures are an expression) is yet to occur at the end of the age (Rom. 8:21–23). To see this from the perspective of the kingdom and its relationship to the new creation, as Christians obey God's mandate to his image bearers to steward all their labors in creation as his representatives (Gen. 1:27–30), they testify to the reality that, in Christ, God has already begun the new creation in them (2 Cor. 5:17; Eph. 4:24), and that the renewal of creation in its outward-bodily forms is yet to come; it will come at the resurrection of the body, in the new heavens and the new earth, when their King returns at the end of this age (1 Cor. 15:25–28; Rev. 21:1–8).

Christ the King, to the hearts and lives of multitudes, to the end of the earth until the end of the age. Its grandeur and glory are seen in the end of the mission envisioned by the apostle John:

> After this I looked, and behold, a great multitude that no one could number, from every nation, from all tribes and peoples and languages, standing before the throne and before the Lamb, clothed in white robes, with palm branches in their hands, and crying out with a loud voice, "Salvation belongs to our God who sits on the throne, and to the Lamb!" And all the angels were standing around the throne and around the elders and the four living creatures, and they fell on their faces before the throne and worshiped God, saying, "Amen! Blessing and glory and wisdom and thanksgiving and honor and power and might be to our God forever and ever! Amen." (Rev. 7:9–12)

However, like those who responded to Christ at Nazareth and Capernaum, the people of God today and their pastors can allow the creep of personal interests and the cares of this present age to make them, as Miller put it, "satisfied with small and occasional contributions of service to this greatest of all causes." If the people of God are to be led into the great kingdom purposes of God for them, particularly through preaching, pastors need to be reminded of and refreshed in the *why* of what they do week after week. Jocko Willink, an ex-military commander who now trains leaders in other fields, recalls the need to have a mission and its cause clear in his own mind before attempting to lead others to execute it. In *Extreme Ownership* Willink writes that before he led a combat mission, the most important question had been answered: Why? Once I analyzed the mission and understood for myself that critical piece of information, I could then believe in the mission. If I didn't believe in it, there was no way I could possibly convince the SEALs in my task unit to believe in it.[20]

Pastors have a far greater *why* than any military commander in history has ever had, and they must own it. The mission in which pastors lead God's people is history defining, global in scope, and cosmically significant. So they must have the great cause to which they lead crystal clear and compellingly in their minds, fueling their affections and aspirations in order to lead as Christ has appointed them.

The apostle Paul set the pace in this (1 Cor. 11:1). The leader of Christ's mission to the Gentiles was openhearted about his affection and aspirations on Christ's mission. In Romans 10:1, just after he disclosed and defended the doctrine of election (Rom. 9:6–24), he revealed what moved his heart: "Brothers, my heart's desire and prayer to God for them is that they may be saved."[21] In 1 Corinthians 9:19–23 he expressed an entrepreneur-like zeal as

---

20 Jocko Willink and Leif Babin, *Extreme Ownership: How U.S. Navy Seals Lead and Win* (New York: St. Martin's, 2017), chap. 3, Kindle.

21 Cf. also Rom. 9:2. John Murray's comments on Rom. 10:1 provide a corrective for those who would use Calvinism as an excuse for complacency on Christ's mission: "Here we have a lesson of profound import. . . . Our attitude to men is not to be governed by God's secret counsel concerning them. It is this lesson and the distinction involved that are so eloquently inscribed on the apostle's *passion* for the salvation of his kinsmen. *We violate the order of human thought and trespass the boundary between God's prerogative and man's when the truth of God's sovereign counsel constrains despair or abandonment of concern for the eternal interests of men.*" John Murray, *The Epistle to the Romans* (Glenside, PA: Westminster Seminary Press, 2022), 376 (emphasis added).

he repeatedly stressed his desire to win all sorts of people to the blessings of the gospel, even at the sacrifice of his own freedoms in custom and comfort (though never compromising the commands of God).[22] And in Acts 20:24, as he faced the certain prospect of suffering, he told the elders at Ephesus, "But I do not account my life of any value nor as precious to myself, if only I may finish my course and the ministry that I received from the Lord Jesus, to testify to the gospel of the grace of God."

In scriptures like these the Holy Spirit has given us a window into the heart of a servant Christ sent to speak for him. His conviction of and contentment with the sovereignty of God did not lead to complacency in the cause of Christ. He fervently aspired to more and more glory for God in the spread of his saving rule to more and more people (cf. 2 Cor. 4:15). Leaders of Christ's church must return repeatedly to the glory, grandeur, and eternity-affecting significance of Christ's cause in order to lead others on it. Archibald Alexander, Samuel Miller's colleague (and founding professor) at Old Princeton, wrote, "If the Christian Church felt her obligations to her Lord and Redeemer as she ought, the whole body would be like a great missionary society, whose chief object was to spread the Gospel over the world."[23]

Conclusion

Before we move on to the principles and practices of pastoral leadership discussed in the rest of this book, it is worth reflecting

---

22 See John Murray, *Principles of Conduct: Aspects of Biblical Ethics* (Grand Rapids, MI: Eerdmans, 1957), 186–89.

23 Archibald Alexander, quoted in David B. Calhoun, *Princeton Seminary*, vol. 1, *Faith and Learning, 1812–1868* (Edinburgh: Banner of Truth, 1994), 139.

on your understanding of and commitment to the mission Christ has committed to his church and has entrusted to your leadership. Do you need to revisit and recommit to the mission on which the Scriptures reveal Christ is leading his church? Does the glory and grandeur of the enterprise you profess to be engaged in still fill your gaze? It must if you are to faithfully steward the appointment Christ has given you as an officer and leader in his kingdom, and which you will find described in the pages that follow.

When George P. Shultz served as secretary of state for the United States, he would invite each newly appointed US ambassador to his office for a meeting. He would spin the globe located in his office and ask the ambassador to point to his or her country. Every time, the new ambassador would point to the country to which he or she had been assigned. Then Shultz would correct the ambassador and say: "*Your* country is the United States. Don't ever forget it."[24] As we will see later on, pastors are Christ's servants sent to speak and lead for him. But, first, in the next chapter we'll see that they have been appointed to their office not by any authority on earth but by the risen King of the cosmos, who is head of the church. The King's method is to send servants of his word to and through his church, and their mission encompasses not any one nation but the entire kingdom of God. We must never forget it!

---

24 Kate Bachelder Odell, "'In the Nation's Service' Review: George Shultz's Quiet Strength," *Wall Street Journal*, March 6, 2023, https://www.wsj.com/articles/in-the-nations-service-review-george-shultzs-quiet-strength-963162d8.

And he gave the apostles, the prophets, the
evangelists, the shepherds and teachers.

EPHESIANS 4:11

·

Nothing is more central or basic than
union and communion with Christ.

JOHN MURRAY

2

The Leadership of a Man of God

Appointed by Christ in Union with Christ

JOHN CALVIN'S pastoral leadership has had an impact on the church for over five hundred years. We may know Calvin as a preacher and theologian. He was this first and foremost, and we will consider the priority he placed on preaching in a subsequent chapter. But we might not appreciate how intentional Calvin was in leading the church to integrate the doctrine he expounded into its life and leadership.

When Calvin returned to Geneva from his exile in Strasbourg, he lamented the dearth of practical implementation of truths being preached from Protestant pulpits. He wrote: "When I first came to this church, it was as good as nothing. They preached, and that was about all. They did indeed go out looking for images and burning them, but in no way was there a reformation. Everything was in a state of confusion."[1] Calvin envisioned the need for

---

1   Herman J. Selderhuis, *John Calvin: A Pilgrim's Life* (Downers Grove, IL: IVP Academic, 2009), 57.

Genevans to put into practice the biblical priorities and patterns he preached, and when he returned to the city on September 13, 1541, he proceeded to "set it in order."[2] He established a biblically constructed presbytery, paying particular attention to "church discipline and organization of church offices."[3] He gave attention to the education of children and youth, and worked to reform the most fundamental of societal institutions, marriage, and more.[4]

Many of the principles and practices that theologically Reformed churches today embrace as givens were, for Calvin and his contemporaries, strategic initiatives in response to God's word. The reformation of the church in the sixteenth century, influenced by Calvin the preacher-theologian, resulted from intentional pastoral leadership that had recovered a biblical vision for the church and developed strategies to intentionally implement biblical priorities in its practice.[5]

John Calvin is a historic example of a man of God, a preacher-leader who intentionally led God's people forward into the vision

2 Theodore Beza, *The Life of John Calvin* (Philadelphia: Westminster Press, 1909), 29.

3 Selderhuis, *John Calvin*, 119. In light of my introductory comments about the pastor as leader serving with fellow elders, it is worth noting that the renewal of the office of elder was pivotal in Calvin's system. "For Calvin elders were the real shepherds since they oversaw the flock." He considered the office of elder "*the* instrument for turning Geneva into a God-pleasing city" (122, emphasis original).

4 Many of the reforms Calvin would lead in Geneva and beyond were first modeled for him by Martin Bucer's leadership in Strasbourg and his writing. See Selderhuis, *John Calvin*, 89. For insight into Bucer's pastoral philosophy, which would have influenced Calvin, see Martin Bucer, *Concerning the True Care of Souls* (Edinburgh: Banner of Truth, 2009). For a compelling picture of Calvin as a preacher-leader and the kinds of strategic initiatives ("reforms") he led, see Selderhuis, *John Calvin*, 179–85.

5 For an appreciative yet candid analysis of Calvin's effectiveness and weaknesses as a leader of the Reformation, see Bruce Gordon, *Calvin* (New Haven, CT: Yale University Press, 2009). Selderhuis summarizes Calvin's vision thus: "improve the world, begin with Geneva." Selderhuis, *John Calvin*, 215.

described in God's word. The underlying conviction of this book is that pastoral leadership is an organic extension of the preaching ministry of a man of God. In the second half of the book we'll see the priority of preaching and how it integrates with the practices of pastoral leadership. But we must first establish what we mean by pastoral leadership.

Definitions and descriptions of leadership in popular pastoral literature can be overly dependent on secular theory and, without careful discernment, introduce unbiblical models and manners into church leadership. They can also be primarily influenced by the unique gifts of a particular author and be too subjective to help those who lack the author's gifts. In this chapter I will offer a definition of pastoral leadership and suggest some biblical foundations for this definition. The goal is to help pastors who are committed to the priority of preaching in ministry to think intentionally, clearly, and principally about their leadership rather than pragmatically or merely expediently. So, if you want to think about your leadership in Christ's cause from biblical and theological precept to wise practice, I invite you to dig in.

Definitions and Foundations

Pastoral leadership is the process where, for the glory of God, a man of God, appointed by the Son of God and empowered by the Spirit of God, proclaims the word of God so that the people of God are equipped to move forward into the purposes of God together.[6]

---

6 Two clarifications might prove helpful at this juncture. (1) The concept of leadership as a process might seem counterintuitive if leadership is defined solely as decision-making and direction setting. Though decision-making and direction setting are integral to the

This definition has developed from the study of biblical passages on church leadership, examples of leadership from history, and a library of publications on leadership theory throughout the course of my pastoral experience. It identifies *the end* to which a pastor is to lead God's people (the purposes of God) and the primary *means* by which he leads to that end (proclamation of the word of God). It also seeks to keep God and his word, the lordship of Christ, and dependence on his Spirit central in pastoral leadership. Each of these aspects will be explained in the chapters that follow. In this chapter we'll look at four precepts that serve as a foundation for this definition.

Christ the King Is Leader of the Church—and Everything Else

No other institution, organization, or movement in history has the place in God's purpose and plan that the church does. This is made compellingly clear in Ephesians 1:20–23. Ephesians 1:15–23 is a record of Paul's prayer for the church that they would apprehend the spiritual blessings that were theirs because of Christ's resurrection. The prayer concludes with a stunning declaration of what the church is: "his body, the fullness of him who fills all in all"

work of leadership, pastoral leadership approaches these functions not as bare assertions of individual will but as the conclusion of a process of discernment that produces wise judgment. (2) Pastoral leadership occurs both in public contexts, with groups or whole congregations, and in private contexts, such as ministry to individuals. While the focus of this book is primarily on the more public leadership of congregations envisioned holistically, the reader should also be able to make thoughtful application of the precepts and practices to the more private and personal circumstances where pastoral leadership is required. Timothy Witmer's treatment of *macro* and *micro* contexts for core shepherding functions is illuminating in this regard. See Timothy Z. Witmer, *The Shepherd Leader: Achieving Effective Shepherding in Your Church* (Phillipsburg, NJ: P&R, 2010).

(1:23). The church is nothing less than the assembly in which the presence and glory of the King of the cosmos dwells! This declaration is grounded in the glorious reality that God raised Christ and enthroned him above all. In verse 19 Paul multiplies superlatives to exalt the immeasurably great, mighty power God exerted to raise Christ. The apostle exults not just in the fact that God raised a dead man to life (as awesome as that is) but also that he seated him *at God's right hand* in the heavenly places (1:20), the place of God's particular favor and power, and of supreme honor and authority (1:20–21). In raising Jesus to this place, God left nothing out of the scope of what Christ is far above or what is under his feet (1:21–22). God enthroned Christ as supreme over every conceivable form of rule. If one can name, conceive, or create a ruler, power, government, or authority in heaven or on earth, God seated Christ over it and placed it under Christ's feet. When God raised Jesus, he enthroned him in the place of his honor, power, and authority over absolutely every created thing and person.

Since Paul had an extensive and intense teaching ministry while in Ephesus (Acts 19:8, 10; 20:20, 27, 31), the Ephesians should have recognized the Old Testament promises he was drawing upon in his prayer. In Ephesians 1:20, "seated him at his right hand" is a direct reference to Psalm 110:1, and Ephesians 1:22, "and he put all things under his feet," refers to Psalm 8:3–6. Both psalms were highpoints in God's unfolding promise of the coming messianic King, who would establish God's rule for God's glory. The apostles preached that this promise was fulfilled in Jesus, whom God had now powerfully raised from the dead as both "Lord and Christ" (Acts 2:36). The stunning declaration of Ephesians 1:23 was grounded in these Old Testament promises. Paul's prayer exults in the fact that God has raised Jesus to the position of universal authority as God's promised eschatological and messianic *King*! And as this King, he has been given to the church as head over all things (1:22). The church holds pride of place in God's purposes as the assembly over which Christ, the King of kings, reigns and which he fills by his Spirit (1:23).

Christ the King Appointed Leaders for His Church—and Some Are Pastors

That Christ has appointed leaders in the church has breathtaking significance, because Ephesians 4:7–16 tells us that pastors are among those Christ the King has commissioned to lead his church. Ephesians 4:8–10 picks up the revelation of Christ from 1:20–23 and pictures him as the victorious King now ascended to the throne of heaven and earth. Ephesians 4:13 makes clear what the King's purpose for his church is. The end that King Jesus intends for his church is that it will be built, as his body, to "mature manhood," which is "the measure of the stature of his fullness." Christ the King's purpose for his body is nothing less than conformity to his image and likeness. Ephesians 4:11–12 show us the means the King has put in place to achieve his purpose. In his victorious ascent, Christ has given gifts meant to equip and build the body toward the end he has prescribed.[7] Verse 11 lists both foundational and continuing gifts, all of which steward God's word.[8] The point to take to heart in terms

---

7 For discussion of how 4:11–12 is interpreted and applied with respect to the equipping function of the pastor-teacher, see chap. 10.

8 I interpret these verses within the framework of a biblical cessationism. Therefore, I take the apostles and the prophets to have been given to lay the foundation of the church

of pastoral leadership is that pastors themselves are among these gifts, appointed by Christ the King to proclaim his word to the end that the church would be led into his purpose.[9] Christ the King leads his people to maturity in his image through preachers he has appointed.[10]

This conviction is reinforced when we consider Paul's farewell to the leaders of the church in Ephesus. Acts 20:17–38 pictures a transition in the order of the church's leadership from one of Christ's foundational leaders (the apostle) to the continuing leaders Christ has appointed, the elders or (as we shall see) pastors. In the apostolic age, the apostles installed elders as leaders of the church (Acts 14:21–23), and elders became standardized as the leaders of the church by the end of the New Testament period (1 Tim. 3:1–2; 5:17; Titus 1:5). However, Acts presents the activities of the apostles as the history of what *Christ*, after his ascension, continued to do by his Spirit (Acts 1:1–2, 8–9).[11] The apostles' acts are, in fact, the acts of the exalted Christ by his Spirit through the apostolic leaders he had appointed (cf. Luke 6:12–16).

---

through the reception and recording of direct revelation (Eph. 2:20; 3:5). Evangelists and pastor-teachers have been given to continue the exposition of that (once-for-all) deposited revelation until the end of the age. For a defense of this position, see Richard B. Gaffin Jr, *Perspectives on Pentecost: New Testament Teaching on the Gifts of the Holy Spirit* (Phillipsburg, NJ: P&R, 1979), 89–116; and Sinclair B. Ferguson, *The Holy Spirit*, Contours of Christian Theology (Downers Grove, IL: InterVarsity Press, 1996), 223–35.

9   The identity of the pastor as a leader will be developed more fully in the next chapter.

10 It is worth noting that the integral relationship of faith, knowledge, and doctrine to the end goal Christ has prescribed for his church (Eph. 4:13) indicates the priority of preaching of the word as the primary means. This will be our topic in chap. 7.

11 See Richard B. Gaffin Jr., *In the Fullness of Time: An Introduction to the Biblical Theology of Acts and Paul* (Wheaton, IL: Crossway, 2022), 59.

When we add to this the plain statement of Acts 20:28 that the group of leaders Paul was addressing was appointed by the Holy Spirit, we see that the appointment of elders for the continuing leadership of Christ's church is no less the gift of Christ the King than are the leaders identified in Ephesians 4:11–12. In fact this group of leaders included the pastors referred to in verse 11. Acts 20:17 identifies the group as the "elders" of the church. However, Acts 20:28 also identifies this same group as "overseers" who are called to "care for" (or shepherd) the church. The text attributes all three of these titles, with their respective functions, to the one group of leaders. They are called "elders" to indicate their spiritual maturity and standing as spiritual fathers, and "overseers" to indicate that they have been entrusted with the stewardship of Christ's people; and they are shepherds (pastors) because they feed, protect, and lead Jesus's flock to the green pastures he has purchased and prepared for them.[12] Christ the King has himself appointed the leadership of his church, and he has appointed pastors, or elders and overseers, to shepherd his people.[13]

12 Cf. 1 Tim. 3:1–2; 5:17; 1 Pet. 5:1–2, where all three terms are attributed to the same office of leaders. The position presented here represents what is traditionally called a "two (and a half) office view." Properly held, this view recognizes the distinction between the pastor, who has been set apart as a *teaching elder* (or minister), for the ministry of the word and sacrament, and the *ruling elder*, who has been set apart to govern the church with a plurality of elders and the pastor.

13 The scope of this book does not permit proper treatment of the office of deacon also appointed by Christ to work in vital partnership with pastoral leadership in the mission of the church (Acts 6:1–6; 1 Tim. 3:8–13). For worthy treatment of this honorable and essential office, see Cornelis Van Dam, *The Deacon: Biblical Foundations for Today's Ministry of Mercy* (Grand Rapids, MI: Reformation Heritage, 2016); and Guy Prentiss Waters, *How Jesus Runs the Church* (Phillipsburg, NJ: P&R, 2011), 96–104.

Christ the King Appointed Leaders Who Are
United to Him—and Are to Imitate Him

The leaders Christ has given to his church are not only appointed by him but also united to him so that he dwells and works in and through them by his Spirit. Pastors are *sons* before they are *stewards* (Rom. 8:14–15; Gal. 4:6–7; Eph. 1:5).[14] By the grace of God, believers are united to Christ, by the Spirit, so that Christ and all the benefits of his saving work are now theirs. This means that Christ is both *for us* and *in us*. In Christ, God has acquitted believers of their guilt and accepts them as righteous, not for any righteousness they have done or will do, but solely on the ground of Christ's righteousness imputed to them for their justification (Rom. 3:21–26; 4:22–25; 5:1, 18–19; 2 Cor. 5:21; Phil. 3:8–9).[15] Union with Christ means also that Christ, by his Spirit, has taken up residence in the believer's inner self and is working to conform his people to his likeness (Rom. 8:9–10, 29; 2 Cor. 3:17–18; Gal. 2:20; Phil. 2:12; cf. 1 Cor. 15:45). Not only has he sanctified believers, delivering them from the dominion and rule of sin (Rom. 6:6–14; 1 Cor. 1:2; Gal. 5:24; Eph. 4:20–24; Col. 1:13); he is sanctifying them.[16] Christ in believers is transforming them progressively, though not yet perfectly, into his image until

14 Timothy Witmer expresses this same fundamental fact by stressing that the identity of the under-shepherd is, first of all, "a sheep." Witmer, *The Shepherd Leader*, 163.

15 Cf. the Westminster Shorter Catechism 33: "Justification is an act of God's free grace, wherein he pardoneth all our sins, and accepteth us as righteous in his sight, only for the righteousness of Christ imputed to us, and received by faith alone."

16 For a thorough treatment of sanctification in its definitive and progressive aspects represented here, see Sinclair B. Ferguson, *Devoted to God: Blueprints for Sanctification* (Edinburgh: Banner of Truth, 2016), esp. 71–91, 241–56; and John Murray, *Collected Writings of John Murray*, vol. 2, *Select Lectures in Systematic Theology* (Edinburgh: Banner of Truth, 1977), 277–317; Murray, *Redemption Accomplished and Applied* (Grand

they will finally be like him, in glory (Rom. 8:23–25, 30; Phil. 3:10–14; Col. 1:27–28). This means that the believer's entire life, as a son of God in Christ, is the pursuit of progress in *imitation of Christ in union with Christ* (Rom. 6:11, 13; 13:14; Eph. 2:10; 4:13, 20–24; Col. 3:1–4, 5, 12, 17).[17]

The point of including this (ridiculously brief) summary of the believer's union with Christ in a book on pastoral leadership is that this glorious gospel reality is also foundational to the identity of every Christian pastor. This is so obvious, it seems unnecessary to mention it; but, sadly, pastors often allow this fundamental reality to fade to the periphery of their consciousness and conduct. The fact that a man of God is, first and foremost, united to Christ has transformative implications not only for his life but also for his leadership. Because a man of God has been appointed by Christ the King and is united to him, he should desire and discipline himself to exemplify Christ in all his stewardship for him. This means imitating both Christ's character *and* his kingly competencies as a leader. I will address the imperative for Christlike character in chapter 5, but what is perhaps underappreciated is how a pastor's union with Christ can also bear fruit in his growth in core competencies of leadership. This key concept will heavily influence this book. A man of God must imitate Christ the King in his competencies as a leader.[18]

Rapids, MI: Eerdmans, 1955), 140–50; and Murray, *Principles of Conduct: Aspects of Biblical Ethics* (Grand Rapids, MI: Eerdmans, 1957), 202–28.

17 I am indebted to Eric Watkins for this summary phrase. See Eric B. Watkins, *The Drama of Preaching: Participating with God in the History of Redemption* (Eugene, OR: Wipf and Stock, 2016), 121–34.

18 More could be said here about the image of Christ and the extension of his rule through every believer (see chap. 1). The argument that follows is, all of this being true of every

Christ the King's Appointed Leaders Seek to
Imitate His Character—and Competencies

Isaiah 11:1–2 provides a compelling portrait of the competencies that would be infallibly possessed by the messianic King whom God promised to his people. God's people had been led into a disastrous cycle of idolatrous disobedience by kings who were, with rare exceptions, unrighteous, unwise, and ineffective. When Assyria loomed near the nation's border as the instrument of God's judgment, Isaiah 11:1–2 promised a future ruler from the royal line of David who would be all that the nation's kings had failed to be.

E. J. Young explains what this portrait of the ideal Davidic King would have meant to the Hebrew reader. Young points out that the couplings listed in 11:2 would have been understood as characteristics necessary for the King. They disclosed the King's *theoretical ability* ("wisdom and understanding"), his *practical ability* ("counsel and might"), and his controlling *motive* ("knowledge and the fear of the LORD"). Young expounds "wisdom and understanding" as the ability to make right decisions at the right time for the right reasons, "counsel and might" as the ability to develop and execute a plan to put these right decisions into action, and the "knowledge and the fear of the LORD" as the personal piety that results from reverence for God, which is the root out of which the King's knowledge grows and the motive that animates his actions as leader of God's people.[19] God was promising his

---

believer, *how much more* ought the pace be set (as it were) by those whom the King has appointed to lead in his name.

19 See Edward J. Young, *The Book of Isaiah*, vol. 1, *Chapters 1–18* (Grand Rapids, MI: Eerdmans, 1965), 379–87. Young provides the qualification that "none of the terms

people a messianic King who would possess all these qualities with Spirit-endowed perfection (11:1–2).[20] In other words, God promised his people *the consummate leader*, who would decide and direct with perfect insight, who would be powerfully and perfectly able to turn right decisions into right actions, and who would do so for the right reasons through his infallible knowledge of and love for God's character and will.

This is Christ the King, who, as we have seen, is now seated on David's throne (Eph. 1:20–23; cf. Acts 2:34–36; 15:16–17), who has inaugurated and is extending his rule in and through his church, and who has appointed leaders for his church who are also, by the Spirit, united to him. This leads us to the conclusion that the kingly characteristics (competencies) described in Isaiah 11:2 suggest a biblically objectifiable pattern of Christlike competencies into which those appointed to lead in the King's cause should aspire to grow. A man of God should desire to be a mature example of Christ's wisdom and understanding, counsel and might, knowledge and fear of the Lord. The most mature, Christ-imitating preacher is profoundly fallible, since, unlike Christ, he remains fallen and finite. But he should make progress in his abilities to know what ought to be done, his ability to get it done, and his motivation in doing so. He should discipline himself for growth in the competencies to make right decisions,

---

employed is entirely exclusive of the others," nor is the description "exhaustive of the messiah's enablement." To this end, he cites John Calvin: "He does not mention, therefore," says Calvin, "all the gifts which were bestowed on Christ, for that was unnecessary; but only shows briefly that Christ came not empty-handed, but well supplied with all gifts, that he might enrich us with them" (379).

20 See chap. 4 on the Spirit's anointing of Christ and the implications for those who lead in union with him.

for the right reasons, and turn those right decisions into right actions.[21] In other words, the *wisdom of Christ* the leader should and can be progressively imaged in a pastor's stewardship of the leadership for which Christ has appointed him.[22]

One of the challenges in equipping pastors to lead is that they can think of wisdom in predominantly theoretical or philosophical terms. Wisdom can be seen solely as the cognitive ability to grasp and expound deep biblical and theological truths. While biblical wisdom requires nothing less than mature knowledge of the Scriptures, the biblical idea combines both cognition and competency. As Herman Bavinck describes it, in the Bible wisdom "characterizes the conduct of those who make the right use of their greater store of knowledge and match the best *means* to the best *ends*."[23] Charles Hodge sees the same practical orientation in the biblical idea of wisdom: "Wisdom and knowledge are intimately related. The former is manifested in the selection of *proper ends*, and of the *proper means* for the accomplishment of those ends."[24] Both

---

21 See Young, *The Book of Isaiah*, 1:382.

22 Three important considerations must be kept in mind, given this application: (1) The main point of this text is to reveal Jesus Christ, who, as King, is the righteous Judge who himself took the righteous judgment for his people so that they are now, in him, judged righteous (Isa. 53:4–6, 11). (2) Christ is *the* promised leader, *the* King whose wise and righteous direction and decisions God's people follow (Matt. 28:20; Luke 6:46; Phil. 2:9–12). (3) The gifts of wisdom given by the Spirit, in union with this Christ, are the privilege and possession of *every* believer and should be expressed in the stewardship of all of life by all Christians (1 Cor. 1:30; Eph. 1:8, 17; Col. 1:9; 3:17). Once again, my point here is, these implications being true of all believers, *how much more* should they be maturely manifest in those whom the King has appointed to lead his people.

23 Herman Bavinck, *Reformed Dogmatics*, ed. John Bolt, trans. John Vriend, vol. 2, *God and Creation* (Grand Rapids, MI: Baker Academic, 2004), 203 (emphasis added).

24 Charles Hodge, *Systematic Theology*, 3 vols. (New York: Scribner, Armstrong, 1872), 1:401 (emphasis added).

Bavinck's and Hodge's descriptions of wisdom occur in contexts where they are discussing wisdom as an attribute of God. One contemporary theologian describes it this way:

> Divine wisdom has in view God's ability (i.e., power) to act for *a right end*. The end reveals not only his wisdom but also *the means* that lead to that end. By his knowledge God discerns things, and by his wisdom, he acts on such understanding. Knowledge concerns the theoretical and wisdom the practical. . . .
>
> God displays his wisdom not only in creation but also in his works of providence, whereby he guides and directs all things to their proper end.[25]

Divine wisdom is expressed in determining *ends*, determining the *means* to reach those ends, and directing *things* according to those means to those ends. This divine wisdom is most fully revealed in Christ (Isa. 11:2; 1 Cor. 1:24, 30; 2 Cor. 4:4; Col. 2:3), to whom a man of God is united by the Spirit. Therefore, the ability to determine right ends and choose right means to attain those ends images the wisdom of God, in whose image we have been created, and it imitates Christ, in union with whom we have been renewed in God's image (Eph. 4:24). The ability to envision a proper end, choose proper means to meet that end, and execute a plan toward that end is, quite simply, *wisdom* in imitation of Christ, in union with Christ. Such wisdom should progressively (though not

---

25 Mark Jones, *God Is: A Devotional Guide to the Attributes of God* (Wheaton, IL: Crossway, 2017), 158–59 (emphasis added).

yet perfectly) be evidenced in the competencies of those Christ has appointed to lead his church.

Implications for Pastoral Leadership

Christ-imitating preachers won't leave their "greater store of knowledge"[26] of God's word at the theoretical or philosophical level. They will apply it to envision the ends, employ the means, and execute the plans of action that will move God's people forward into God's purposes for them. In leadership parlance, this is identified as the ability to capture and communicate *vision* (ends) and develop and execute *strategy* (means). Vision is simply a clearly discerned view of the end to which God would lead his people in the particular place and time in which he has appointed a man of God to lead them. Strategy is the intentional definition and employment of the means God has prescriptively (through his word) and providentially provided to lead his people to the end envisioned. To lead God's people in the context where Christ has appointed him, the pastor must learn how to communicate a biblical vision and define a biblical strategy. Alongside the Christlike character required to serve as an example for God's people, the abilities to communicate vision and define and execute strategy are core competencies in which the leaders of God's people must continue to grow.

Conclusion

In this chapter we have seen that Christ the King has appointed pastors to lead his church with Christ-imitating wisdom to

---

26 Bavinck, *Reformed Dogmatics*, 2:203.

communicate direction for the people of God (vision) and make decisions on how to get them there (strategy). In the second half of this book, we'll see how this can (and must) be done primarily through the word preached. This is why we have begun by defining pastoral leadership as "the process where, for the glory of God, a man of God, appointed by the Son of God and empowered by the Spirit of God, proclaims the word of God so that the people of God are equipped to move forward into the purposes of God together." I would argue that this is historically what men of God such as Calvin did. While they might not have used contemporary leadership parlance, they had clear insight into the consequences of the word they preached for the community and time in which they served, and they developed and deployed the means to effectively lead the people they served into those consequences. However, in order for these principles to become practice in a pastor's leadership, he must first be clear about who he is in God's purposes and process with God's people. He must have the conviction that as a preacher he is a leader in Christ's cause. It is to his identity as a preacher-leader, a man of God, that we turn next.

But as for you, O man of God, flee these things.

1 TIMOTHY 6:11

*All scripture is breathed out by God and
profitable . . . that the man of God may be
complete, equipped for every good work.*

2 TIMOTHY 3:16–17

*Pastoral leadership is the process where, for the glory
of God, a man of God, appointed by the Son of God
and empowered by the Spirit of God, proclaims the
word of God so that the people of God are equipped
to move forward into the purposes of God together.*

3

The Identity of a Man of God

The Preacher-Leader

AMBASSADORS LEAD. George C. Marshall is a historic example of ambassadorial leadership. Formerly the general responsible for rebuilding the US army in preparation for World War II and leading it as chief of staff through the war, Marshall was asked by President Truman to put his leadership skills to work in the field of diplomacy as secretary of state (1947–1949). Marshall's competency for both persuasion and action, turning "mere ideas . . . into fact,"[1] resulted in the Marshall Plan, which rescued Europe from economic and social disaster after the war and protected the United States' strategic interests abroad. Marshall was never the head of government for the United States, but as its senior ambassador he led on behalf of the government,

---

1 Lance Morrow, "George Marshall: The Last Great American?," *Smithsonian*, August 1997, cited in Jack Uldrich, *Soldier, Statesman, Peacemaker: Leadership Lessons from George C. Marshall* (New York: AMACOM, 2005), 65.

through word and deed, as he represented his nation to other nations. Ambassadors are servants of the head of state or the sovereign who sent them, but as stewards of their leader, ambassadors lead their state's mission to other states.[2] They are officials appointed by their government to speak and act on its behalf in order to persuade allies or adversaries to align with the interests of their state.[3]

Sent to Bring the Word of God

Pastoral leadership is ambassadorial. Pastors have been set apart and sent by Christ the King to bring his word to his adversaries (those yet outside his kingdom) and his allies (subjects of his kingdom). The pastor's brief is to persuade those to whom he speaks to align with his sovereign's agenda. He does this primarily through the means of preaching. But understanding who he is as a preacher, who his King has appointed him to be, can inspire a pastor's aspirations and expectations for the faithful stewardship of his calling. In this chapter we'll look at some related biblical terms and titles that combine to show us that a pastor, because he is a preacher, is a leader. He is a man of God sent with the word of God to lead the people of God into the purposes of God.

---

2 For example, the United States Mission to the United Nations website lists ambassadors as "mission leaders." https://usun.usmission.gov/our-leaders/.

3 For example, the concern of former ambassador Eric Rubin regarding the lack of appointees to ambassadorial posts in 2022 was because an ambassador is "the personal representative of the president of the United States and he carries the president's authority." Annie Linskey and Ken Thomas, "Biden's Picks for Some Ambassador Posts Remain Stalled," *Wall Street Journal*, December 28, 2022, https://www.wsj.com/articles/bidens-picks-for-some-ambassador-posts-remain-stalled-11672242409.

Sent as Pastor

Pastor is a title that is inherently about leadership. We have seen already that Christ, in his triumphant ascent as King of the cosmos (Eph. 4:8–10), gave gifts to his church for the *purpose* that the body would be built to maturity, evidenced particularly by conformity to Christ's character, stability in the truth, and properly working together for the body's continued growth (Eph. 4:13–16). For this purpose, Christ appointed pastors. What is sometimes overlooked in discussions of pastoral leadership is that leadership is inherent in the title *pastor*. Ephesians 4:11 is the only occurrence of the noun *pastor* ("shepherd," ESV) in the New Testament.[4] The image of a shepherd, at its simplest, is of one who moves sheep from one destination to another for (at least) their protection and provision. In other words, inherent in the title *pastor* is the wisdom to know *where* the flock should go and *how* to get the sheep to where they should go, and the competency to effectively guide them there. In terms of God's flock this involves, at a most basic level, persuading people to move from where they currently are to the green pastures of God's plan and purpose.

The fact that Paul didn't explain the term *pastor* in his only usage of it indicates that he expected his readers to intuitively

---

4   Pastor (*poimēnas*). Ernest Best writes, "It is better to translate this as 'shepherds' rather than the normal rendering 'pastors'; in this way we retain the original underlying image and avoid all the overtones surrounding the modern use 'pastor.'" Ernest Best, *Essays on Ephesians* (Edinburgh: T&T Clark, 1997), 167. While I prefer to retain the term *pastor* for common use, I follow Best's linguistic rationale (see below) and have sympathy with his concern about the cultural overtones. As one pastor put it to me, "When people hear the word *pastor* they tend to think 'chaplain.'" Or as I recall hearing it reported, Dr. Lloyd-Jones once opined that most congregations don't want a pastor; they want a "pet lamb."

understand its meaning, either from Paul's previous teaching (cf. Acts 20:28) or from its cultural associations (or both). Some have persuasively argued that the image of the shepherd in the ancient Near East was a common picture of leadership, and this leadership was expressed fundamentally through protecting and providing for and feeding the flock.[5] Timothy Witmer has developed this conclusion from a biblical-theological perspective, locating the notion of shepherding as leadership in God's shepherd-leadership of Israel (Gen. 48:15; Pss. 80:1; 95:6–7).[6] Given that God's leadership of his people was typified through the leadership of King David (1 Sam. 13:14; 2 Sam. 5:2; Ps. 78:70–72), we should not be surprised that the leadership gifts we saw given in Ephesians 4:11 were presented as the consequence of Christ's victorious ascent to the Davidic throne (cf. Ps. 68:18; Eph. 1:20–23). When Paul speaks in Ephesians 4:11 of Christ giving pastors, the title reveals that David's greater son, now exalted as King of all, has given *under-shepherd–leaders* to his people. Pastor means leader.

John Calvin believed that leadership was basic to the identity of the pastor. In his exposition of 1 Timothy 3:1 Calvin describes the New Testament overseer, or bishop (*episkopēs*), as a leader. According to Calvin, " 'Pastor,' 'bishop,' 'priest,'—these in Scripture are taken for one, that is to say, for those who are called in the Church of God to *teach and govern* his household."[7] For Calvin, the pastor, precisely because he is a teacher of God's word, has

---

5   See Timothy S. Laniak, *Shepherds after My Own Heart: Pastoral Traditions and Leadership in the Bible* (Downers Grove, IL: InterVarsity Press, 2006), 31–114.

6   See Timothy Z. Witmer, *The Shepherd Leader: Achieving Effective Shepherding in Your Church* (Phillipsburg, NJ: P&R, 2010), 11–12.

7   John Calvin, quoted in T. H. L. Parker, *Calvin's Preaching* (Louisville: Westminster John Knox, 1992), 36 (emphasis added).

a governing or leadership function. But it is always exercised in submission to and through the word of God. He writes:

> Boldly dare all for God's Word, and force every power, fame, wisdom and highness to submit to the majesty of the Word and to be obedient to it; supported by the power of the Word, to command all, from the highest to the lowest; to build up the house of Christ, to overturn that of Satan; to pasture the flock, to tear apart the wolves; to educate and spur on the teachable; to punish, rebuke and subdue the rebellious and obstinate; and finally, if necessary, to break out with words of thunder and hurl verbal lightning bolts. But *everything through the Word of God.*[8]

This emphasis on the pastor calling others, even authorities, to submit to God's will through the means of God's word brings us back to the concept of ambassadorial leadership.

Sent as Ambassador

In 2 Corinthians 5:20 Paul identifies himself and his apostolic cohort as ambassadors.[9] The term he uses for ambassador (*presbeuō*) identifies "a representative of a ruling authority." In this sense an ambassador was one who was commissioned to represent his sender on a special

---

8 John Calvin, *Institutes* 4.8.9, quoted in Herman J. Selderhuis, *John Calvin: A Pilgrim's Life* (Downers Grove, IL: IVP Academic, 2009), 242 (emphasis added).

9 This text is often applied to believers in general to emphasize, rightly, the privilege and responsibility that all Christians have to minister the truth of the gospel in evangelism and in the mutual edification of other believers (see chap. 10). However, this is an application by implication. Paul's primary intent and focus is to describe and defend his particular ministry as a set-apart and sent servant of the word.

assignment and exercised the authority of the one who sent him.[10] In Paul's case he fulfilled his ambassadorial commission by *speaking* on behalf of Christ, who sent him as he sought to persuade those to whom he had been sent (2 Cor. 5:11). Paul expected that when he communicated the word, God effected his will through the message (2 Cor. 3:3) because, when the ambassador spoke as Christ's sent servant, none less than God himself made his appeal through him![11]

Paul saw his stewardship, as a servant of the word, as an ambassador sent to persuade people to align with his Master's will. Calvin emphasized the preacher's identity as an ambassador when he expounded 2 Corinthians 5:20:

> When a man is the envoy of his prince and has complete authority to do what is committed to his charge, he will so to say borrow the prince's name. He will say, "We are doing this; we instruct; we have commanded; we want that done." Now, when he speaks like this, he is not intending to take anything from his master. So it is with God's servants. They know that God has ordained them as instruments and that he employs them in his service in such a way that they do nothing by their own power; it is the Master who leads them.[12]

Sent as Herald

The concept of an ambassador is also related to the idea of a herald. In the ancient period, servants who had a loud, clear voice were

---

10 See Murray J. Harris, *The Second Epistle to the Corinthians: A Commentary on the Greek Text*, The New International Greek Testament Commentary (Grand Rapids, MI: Eerdmans, 2005), 445.

11 Cf. Rom. 1:1, 5; 10:15–17; 1 Cor. 4:1. See chap. 7 for a fuller development of this concept.

12 John Calvin, in Parker, *Calvin's Preaching*, 27.

sometimes sent by a ruler or a state to announce news, such as calling soldiers to assemble for battle or citizens to assemble as the *ecclessia*. Heralds could serve as auctioneers, be middlemen in the marketplace, or announce judicial verdicts. Heralds were also sent as political ambassadors or to serve with them. A herald might wear a livery or carry a staff to indicate that he was an official of the master who sent him. But what distinguished the herald was that he was always under and represented the authority of his sender and that he announced his message with a loud clear voice.[13] In the biblical period the term used for this kind of servant was *kēryx*. This is significant for our topic because, even though the noun *kēryx* is used sparingly in the New Testament, Paul chooses it in 1 Timothy 2:7 and 2 Timothy 1:11 to describe his appointment as a *preacher*. He then chooses the verb (*kēryssō*), which the New Testament uses much more frequently,[14] in 2 Timothy 4:2 when he charges Timothy to *preach* the word. In the New Testament the preacher is a herald (*kēryx*), and to preach (*kēryssō*) is to herald God's word. The preacher serves as an ambassador appointed to announce the word of his Master clearly and with his authority. Pastors, as preachers, are Christ's sent servants who proclaim his will with his authority and summon others to respond to it.

Sent as Man of God

This final charge to Timothy, to herald the word (2 Tim. 4:2), is given in the context of our final title, which forms a dominant

13   See Lothar Coenen, "κηρύσσω," in *The New International Dictionary of New Testament Theology*, ed. Colin Brown, 4 vols. (Grand Rapids, MI: Zondervan, 1975–1978), 3:48–57.

14   Sixty-one times. See Coenen, "κηρύσσω," 52.

theme for this book, *man of God* (2 Tim. 3:17; cf. 1 Tim. 6:11). It is a definitive and compelling title attributed to stewards of God's word in the Scriptures and, coming as it does in the Pastoral Epistles, provides insight into how the apostle viewed the preachers who would continue the mission in the post-apostolic age (cf. 2 Tim. 2:2). Jonathan Griffiths has demonstrated that the title finds its Old Testament background in the way Moses was identified before his death: "This is the blessing with which Moses *the man of God* blessed the people of Israel before his death" (Deut. 33:1; cf. Josh 14:6; 1 Chron. 23:14).[15] *Man of God* was used also of David (2 Chron. 8:14; Neh. 12:24–36) in his function as king of Israel ordering the worship of Israel, of Samuel (1 Sam. 9:6–10) in his function as prophet and judge of Israel, of Elijah and Elisha (1 Kings 17:18, 24; 2 Kings 1:9–13; 4:7, 27; 5:8, 14–20) and of several other anonymous prophets (e.g., 1 Sam. 2:27; 1 Kings 13:1, 5, 8, 11–13; 20:28). As Paul concludes his ambassadorial leadership of Christ's mission to the Gentiles, he calls Timothy to accept responsibility for the stewardship to which he is appointed; Paul's language connects Timothy's identity to Israel's prophetic leadership all the way back to Moses, the prototypical prophet-leader.

Deuteronomy 18:18 sheds light on the place of the man of God and his priorities in the realization of God's purposes. This verse provides us with what E. J. Young calls the "essential nature of the prophetic function."[16] Precisely because it envi-

---

15 See Jonathan I. Griffiths, *Preaching in the New Testament: An Exegetical and Biblical-Theological Study*, New Studies in Biblical Theology (Downers Grove, IL: IVP, 2017), 58–59.

16 Edward J. Young, *My Servants the Prophets* (Grand Rapids, MI: Eerdmans, 1952), 57.

sions *the prophet* who will supersede all others in fidelity and efficacy, it summarizes the core assignment for God's appointed spokesmen, "And I will put my words in his mouth, and he shall speak to them all that I command him." Young's survey of this and other passages[17] demonstrates that the function of the prophet is "declaring the word which God has given . . . speaking forth a message which has been received from a superior"; and "as far as the prophets were concerned the superior was God himself."[18] This is akin to the function and role attributed in the New Testament to the ambassador and preacher (herald).

However, the Old Testament man of God, precisely as he fulfilled his prophetic function, also fulfilled a leadership role. Moses's commission was to "bring out" Israel from Egypt (Ex. 6:6, 26) by "tell[ing]" Pharaoh all that YHWH said to him (Ex. 6:29). Moses served as Israel's prototypical judge, exercising what would later become the kingly responsibility of making right decisions for the people according to the word of God (Ex. 18:13; cf. Isa. 11:1–2).[19] The same was true of Samuel as the man of God (1 Sam. 9:6). He judged Israel (1 Sam. 7:15), which included delivering and defending God's people (1 Sam. 7:12–13) as well as proclaiming God's word. Israel expected that a king would judge them, as well as fight for them (1 Sam. 8:6, 19–20), a role that was filled, again in typical fashion, by David as the man of God (1 Sam. 17:45–53; 2 Sam. 7:8–9; 8:15;

---

17 Cf., e.g., Ex. 4:15, 16; 7:1; Isa. 30:2; Jer. 1:17; 15:19.

18 Young, *My Servants the Prophets*, 59–60.

19 Note that the problem in Ex. 18 was not that Moses was performing judgments (v. 22) but that he was trying to do it alone (vv. 13–18).

Ps. 78:72). As we saw in the last chapter, this was consummately fulfilled by the final, faithful, flawless King from David's line (Isa. 11:1–5). The priority of the Old Testament man of God was to receive and deliver God's word, and he was to apply that word in decision and action to lead the people of God into the promised purposes of God. Once again, this is akin to the stewardship Paul entrusts to Timothy as he puts the church in order through the preaching of the word (1 Tim. 1:3; 3:1–15; 5:3–25; 2 Tim. 4:2).

This is not an argument for a straight line of continuity between the Old Testament prophet and the New Testament pastor. Preachers, in the post-apostolic period, now proclaim God's word not by receiving direct revelation but by expounding the revelation contained in the Scriptures. Edmund Clowney qualifies it this way: "As we preach the Word of God we are not clothed in apostolic authority. We cannot bear [the apostles'] eyewitness to the risen Christ. But by God's grace we are numbered among those faithful men into whose hands the apostolic deposit has been placed."[20] However, in order to function as those "faithful men" (2 Tim. 2:2), pastors should appreciate and embrace the analogy between the prophet, the ambassador, the herald, and the man of God.[21] It is precisely as a pastor-teacher devotes himself to the study of the final authoritative and suf-

---

20 Edmund P. Clowney, *Preaching and Biblical Theology* (Grand Rapids, MI: Eerdmans, 1961), 61. Cf. Eph. 2:20; 4:11; Heb. 1:1–2; 2 Pet. 1:16–19.

21 Griffiths is surely correct when he states, "The use of the title 'man of God' indicates that Timothy's preaching ministry will likewise stand in the line of a continuity with the ministries of God's authoritative speakers throughout history." Griffiths, *Preaching in the New Testament*, 60. In fact, for Griffiths, the title *man of God* is "the functional equivalent of the term 'prophet'" (59).

ficient deposit of divine revelation, received by the prophets and apostles (Eph. 2:20) and now contained in the Spirit-inspired Scriptures (2 Tim. 3:16), that God, as it were, puts his word in the mouth of a man of God.[22]

Implications

These terms and titles combine to provide a convincing and compelling portrait of the pastor as a man of God, one who has been appointed to proclaim God's word to lead God's people into God's purposes. So, what difference does it make for a pastor to know that Christ has appointed him to be a man of God in the context in which he has sent him to serve?

Identity and Intention

My wife and I raised two boys. One of our goals was that they would leave our house—not because we didn't like them but because we thought our job was to equip our boys to become men who would be able to lead their own households and serve their churches and communities. At some point my wife decided to inspire her sons toward manhood by assigning Kipling's "If" for their reading. The four stanzas of the famous poem rehearse risks, wounds, and temptations faced in this world, and the virtue needed to overcome them. The final line promises that *if* one can master the virtues, "you'll be a Man, my son!"[23] It's a poetic, albeit somewhat stoic, call

---

22 The nature of the prophet's appointment is perhaps most vividly portrayed in the way Jeremiah understood his calling: "Then the LORD put out his hand and touched my mouth. And the LORD said to me, 'Behold, I have put my words in your mouth'" (Jer. 1:9).

23 Rudyard Kipling, "If" (ca. 1895).

to manhood in the real world that aims to give a young man a sense of identity to which to aspire.[24]

Paul was doing something similar with Timothy when he reminded him of his identity as a man of God (1 Tim. 6:11; 2 Tim. 3:17). In leadership, as in life, you need to know who you are, who God has appointed you to be, before you know what you are to do. A renewed appreciation of the pastor's identity as a man of God should result in intentional attitudes and actions, such as seeking God through his word and submitting oneself and stewardship to God's word.

Seeking God and Studying His Word

Being a man of God means you are God's man. That means you must be deeply familiar with God and his will through his word.

I remember visiting a Palestinian church in the old city of Jerusalem. As we entered the room where we were to worship, we walked past the pastor just leaving his "office." I noticed that the sign on the door (which had an English translation) read "The Prophet's Chamber." I don't know what that group of believers understood about foundational and continuing gifts, but I recall thinking how much better that sign reflected the pastor's identity and function than the professionalized and corporate "office." The point is that whatever a pastor chooses to name his designated workspace, his work should be characterized by meetings with God.[25] A man of God carves out the time and space to seek God

---

24 The boys gained huge points one Christmas by returning a hand-written version of the poem to their mother as part of a Christmas gift!

25 I have been told that A. W. Tozer insisted on his room being called his "study" for similar reasons.

and to increase in his knowledge of God. This is not the same as merely studying to mine more information *about* God. Too many pastors preach as though they know God only by reputation rather than as *their* God, whom they love and trust, and with whom they walk in communion. In order to make God and his purposes known and to lead people into those purposes, a man of God must know the one for whom he speaks.

This, of course, is attained only through the study of God's word. Studying to prepare for the pulpit is of highest priority for a man of God. But his study of God's word must go beyond merely preparing for the next teaching he is required to deliver. Because the Bible is where God speaks today, God's man must know it, understand it, breathe it, and bleed it. For all the advantages of digital information platforms, they are no substitute for the pastor's personal study of God's word written, and they can, in fact, supplant it through their ease of access and functionality as pastors multitask word-related activities. Contemporary pastors can deceive themselves that they are studying the word when they are merely amassing information about issues related (perhaps) to the word. In order to be who he has been appointed to be and to do what he has been appointed to do, a man of God must be a man of God's book.

Submission and Stewardship

A man of God is like a butler, not the lord of the manor. God's man doesn't own God's house, but he has been entrusted with the stewardship of it. This means he must both reverently accept limits to his authority *and* accept his responsibilities and be disciplined in them. A subtle and insidious temptation often plagues church leaders who have gifts, passion, and experience in leadership. Because leaders must genuinely own their mission if they are to have any hope of executing it well, they can start to believe it is "*my* mission" and "*my* church."[26] The grievous consequences of this psychology among pastors are seen in far too many wounded and fractured churches. I will say more about this when we consider the character of a man of God. Suffice it to say here that a pastor who understands he is *a man of God* and not *the man* understands he is the servant and not the sovereign. Therefore, he commits himself to leading in submission to God and the authorities God has prescribed in his word.

This is why a man of God is committed to leading with the other leaders Christ has appointed for his church. As we saw in chapter 2, Christ has appointed a plurality of elders, among whom are pastors who together share the stewardship of leading the people of God. To emphasize leadership by the pastor, as this book does, does not mean the pastor leads alone or above the other elders of the church. A man of God understands that he is not a prelate or pope, but, as someone set apart to preach God's word, he leads with his fellow elders as together they make decisions and set direction for Christ's church.[27]

Far from mitigating the pastor's responsibility and role in leadership, God's design of plurality and parity of elders heightens it. Precisely because he has been set apart for the stewardship of God's word, a man of God has a primary responsibility to lead the leader-

---

26 This could be as much a temptation for church leaders who are not pastors, particularly if they do own the enterprises they are accustomed to leading. The same rights and, therefore, approaches to the execution of leadership do not necessarily apply to the stewardship of Christ's church.

27 The order and polity of how officers of the church lead together are beyond the scope of this book. However, for a description of consultative and collaborative decision-making and direction setting in the context of a plurality of elders, see chap. 9.

ship process of the church. As he honors the office entrusted to other leaders by consulting and collaborating with them, the pastor has the privilege and responsibility to communicate the vision and define the strategies for the church that he sees in Scripture. As a pastor he must earnestly seek to lead the people God has entrusted to him into greener pastures. As an ambassador he must labor to lead the people to whom God has sent him to align with God's purposes. And as a herald he must lead them there through the preaching of God's Word. He has been appointed by the Son of God to proclaim the word of God to lead the people of God into the purposes of God. This is the summons to which a man of God must respond and the stewardship in which he must be intentional, disciplined, and growing in competence.

Conclusion

It is foundational for pastoral leadership that the pastor knows who he is in God's purposes. But it is more fundamental for him to remember *whose* he is. We have seen that the Christian pastor is a son in Christ before he is the servant of Christ, and that it is just as important for the pastor to remember that he is *a* man of God, not *the* man of God. He serves the mission united to and following the leadership of the Christ who alone fulfilled Deuteronomy 18:18 and who was sent, as *the herald*, to lead God's people into their spiritual liberty by proclaiming the good news to them (Luke 4:18–19).[28] Christ the King himself continues to lead the extension of his kingdom through the proclamation of his word by the gifts he has given (Eph. 4:16). The contemporary man of God follows

---

28 The idea of the *kēryx* was integral to Jesus's own sense of messianic identity and mission. I will develop the priority of preaching in Jesus's leadership of his kingdom in chap. 7.

and depends on Christ, *the man of God par excellence*, who had the anointing of the Spirit without measure to fulfill his appointment (Luke 4:18; John 3:34) and has now poured out that same Spirit on the servants he has sent. This is the next foundational principal for pastoral leadership. Christ has not only *appointed* pastors to lead in his church; he has *anointed* them with power for their stewardship. It is to this essential dynamic of the Spirit's power for pastoral leadership that we turn in the next chapter.

———

Before moving on, take some time to reflect on your own stewardship in light of this chapter.

1. Prayerfully review Scripture texts that speak directly about the pastor's identity (e.g., 2 Cor. 5:20; Eph. 4:11; 2 Tim. 3:17).

2. Revisit your call to the ministry, your sense of it, and the circumstances surrounding it. Were there key Scripture texts or crucial voices (e.g., pastors or elders) that God used?

3. Evaluate how you are stewarding your Christ-appointed identity:
   - Are you preaching the Scriptures with their God-given authority?
   - Are you managing your responsibilities and the expectations of others as though you are your own man, someone else's man, or God's man?
   - How are you relating to other Christ-appointed leaders in your church? Are you honoring their office? Are you capitulating on convictions?

- Do you hope and expect to take anyone anywhere with your preaching? Or are you contenting yourself with merely conveying information?

My speech and my message were not in plausible words of wisdom, but in demonstration of the Spirit and of power.

1 CORINTHIANS 2:4

O for the Spirit of God to make and keep us alive unto God, faithful to our office, and useful to our generation.

CHARLES SPURGEON

4

The Power for a Man of God

The Fullness of the Holy Spirit

ARCHIBALD ALEXANDER taught pastors to aspire to and expect effectiveness in their stewardship of Christ's cause.[1] When he was entrusted with delivering the pastoral charge at a former student's ordination service, the Old Princeton pastor of pastors said:

> Be much concerned about the success of your ministry! Cry mightily to God, that He would follow your labours with His blessing, and give you precious souls for your hire, and as seals of your mission. . . . Desire success *and expect it*. . . . Do not be elated with prosperity in preaching or depressed when straitened.[2]

---

1   Material in this chapter is adapted from my article "Preaching in the Power of the Holy Spirit: An Ordinary Expectation?," in *The Westminster Theological Journal* 85, no. 1 (2023).

2   A. A. Alexander, quoted in James M. Garretson, *Princeton and Preaching* (Carlisle, PA: Banner of Truth, 2005), 120 (emphasis added).

In saying this, Alexander was in concert with the conviction expressed by the Westminster Assembly about the effectiveness of God's word preached. The men of God who collaborated to pen that summary of biblical doctrine expressed their belief about preaching this way: "The Spirit of God maketh the reading, but especially the preaching, of the Word, an *effectual means* of convincing and converting sinners, and of building them up in holiness and comfort, through faith, unto salvation."[3] This conviction is grounded in the Scriptures themselves (cf. Isa. 55:11; Jer. 23:29; Heb. 4:12). Throughout church history men of God have expected that the Spirit of God would powerfully effect the purposes of God in those who hear the word of God preached.

But it is also true that many a pulpit has seemed ineffective in leading churches to the kind of congregational and individual transformation the Scriptures envision from a regular diet of God's word preached. The Puritan Thomas Boston lamented the fruitlessness he viewed as characteristic of the Scottish church in his day. He wrote:

We may call ordinances Ichabod; and name the faithful preachers of Scotland no more Naomi, but Mara, for the Lord deals bitterly with them, in so much forsaking his ordinances as at this day. The Lord hath forsaken them in a great measure, as to success attending their labours. They toil all the night; but little or nothing is caught; few or none can they find to come into the net.[4]

---

3 Westminster Shorter Catechism 89 (emphasis added).
4 Thomas Boston, *The Art of Man Fishing: How to Reach the Lost* (Fearn, Ross-Shire, UK: Christian Focus, 2012), 17.

As Boston assessed his own effectiveness, he applied the lament to himself and attributed at least some of his ineffectiveness to his own condition:

> I fear I may say, I have almost spent my strength in vain, and my labour for nought, for Israel is not gathered. O my soul, what may be the cause of this, *why does my preaching do so little good?* No doubt part of the blame lies on myself, and a great part of it too.[5]

Seasoned and sound men of God have continued to raise Boston's concern in their own times. In the nineteenth century Charles Spurgeon put the question to preaching that lacked the weight of "the divine influence," which gives it divine energy and power.[6] In the mid-twentieth century William Still posed the same question rather searchingly: "Why is it that one man preaching can bring spiritual light to bear on the sacred page and make the Book live, while another makes it seem like the dullest book on earth?"[7] In turn, Martyn Lloyd-Jones addressed the question of the Spirit's power in his massively influential *Preaching and Preachers.* "The Doctor," as he was frequently called, diagnosed much of the preaching in his day this way: "There is certainly no lack of words; but is there much evidence of power in our preaching?"[8]

---

5 Boston, *The Art of Man Fishing*, 18 (emphasis added).

6 Charles Spurgeon, *Lectures to My Students* (Grand Rapids, MI: Zondervan, 1954), 191–92.

7 William Still, "The Holy Spirit in Preaching," *Christianity Today* 1, no. 23 (1957): 8–10.

8 D. Martyn Lloyd-Jones, *Preaching and Preachers* (Grand Rapids, MI: Zondervan, 1971), 312. I would differ with Lloyd-Jones's view of the baptism of the Spirit; however, I

John Stott then raised the concern in the 1980s when he wrote, "Why, then, does the power of the Spirit seem to accompany our preaching so seldom?"[9]

Today the question is no different. Why does some preaching seem biblically accurate and yet ineffective in leading to any identifiable effect on Christ's mission or in his people? How is it that pastors whose preaching lacks for nothing in terms of orthodox information can remain characteristically ineffective in leading the people they serve forward in the purposes of God?[10] For some the default reply is to attribute ineffectiveness solely to God's sovereign will to work or not in the lives of those to whom Christ has sent them. Without question, a biblical theology of the sovereignty of God affirms that there are seasons and situations in which it has not pleased God to effect any observable response to the preaching of the word in the lives of his people.[11] But the corruption that yet remains in the heart of every saint makes it all too easy, even for pastors,

---

believe his description of the phenomena of "unction" (and its lack) in preaching is accurate, searching, and helpful (see 304–25).

9 John Stott, *Between Two Worlds: The Art of Preaching in the Twentieth Century* (Grand Rapids, MI: Eerdmans, 1982), 329.

10 We must keep in mind that our assessment of effectiveness in pastoral leadership must leave room for our finiteness and fallenness, which affect it. God may indeed be at work in ways we cannot see, and the infallible and final assessment of our stewardship is God's alone (1 Cor. 4:1–5). The danger is that this reality can be co-opted by our yet-corrupted hearts to cover a lack of God-glorifying, neighbor-loving zeal (Rom. 12:8–12) for the stewardship he has entrusted to us.

11 In the purpose of God, he might choose to effect a judicial hardening through the ministry of his word (e.g., Isa. 6:10; Luke 8:9–10; John 12:38–40; 2 Cor. 2:15–16). I will forgo addressing this topic here due to space and the conviction that, ordinarily, in the day of salvation, judicial hardening is not the category by which a man of God motivates himself and assesses whether his ministry has the desired effect (Rom. 10:1; 11:13–14; 1 Cor. 6:2).

to cover up complacency and insulate our comfort zones by assuming that God does not will to work, rather than asking, as Boston did, whether some lack in us hinders effective pastoral leadership.[12]

For Spurgeon the cause of the problem was often clear. "The lack of distinctly recognizing the power of the Holy Ghost lies at the root of many useless ministries."[13] In what follows we'll see that because a man of God has been not only *appointed* but also *anointed* by Christ, he should expect and desire that his stewardship would be accompanied by the Holy Spirit's power. We'll also see that failure to properly relate to the Holy Spirit and intentionally depend on him could be a primary cause of apparent ineffectiveness in pastoral leadership. A brief sketch of the Spirit's relationship to Christ, in his ministry as Messiah, and how this now relates to a man of God will help to clarify the intentional priority that the person, presence, and power of the Holy Spirit should have in the preacher-leader's stewardship.

The Power of the Spirit under Appointment by and in Union with Christ

The anointing with the Spirit of the Lord was central to Jesus's identity as the Christ and, in his office as Messiah, essential to his ability to execute his ministry and inaugurate his kingdom.[14] The

---

12 See Horatius Bonar, *Words to Winners of Souls* (Phillipsburg, NJ: P&R, 1995), 21–23.

13 Spurgeon, *Lectures to My Students*, 195.

14 "At the Jordan, Christ (conceived and so already indwelt by the Spirit; Luke 1:35) received the Spirit *as an endowment for the kingdom task that lay before him*; in his exaltation, he received the Spirit as the reward for that task behind him and successfully completed." Richard B. Gaffin Jr., *In the Fullness of Time: An Introduction to the Biblical Theology of Acts and Paul* (Wheaton, IL: Crossway, 2022), 123 (emphasis

Gospel of Luke records that, prior to Jesus's opening his public ministry in Galilee, the Spirit came upon Jesus at his baptism (3:22). Luke points to this anointing as key to the power in which Jesus exercised his ministry (4:1, 14). Jesus himself refers to the Spirit's anointing as the source of his messianic ministry:

---

added). John Owen writes, "The Holy Spirit, in a peculiar manner, anointed him with all those *extraordinary powers and gifts* which were necessary for the exercise and discharging of his office on the earth." Then, with particular reference to Isa. 61:1 and Christ's use of it in Luke 4, Owen explains: "It is the prophetical office of Christ, and his discharge thereof in his ministry on the earth, which is intended. And he applies these words unto himself with respect unto his preaching of the gospel, Luke 4:18, 19; for this was that office which he principally attended unto here in the world, as that whereby he instructed men in the nature and use of his other offices." John Owen, *The Works of John Owen*, ed. William H. Goold, vol. 3 (Edinburgh: T&T Clark, n.d.), 171 (emphasis original). The Westminster Confession of Faith, as it affirms both the divine and human natures of Jesus, explains that Jesus's anointing with the Spirit was in order that he would be equipped, according to his human nature, to execute his ministry. "The Lord Jesus, in his human nature thus united to the divine, was sanctified, and anointed with the Holy Spirit, above measure, having in him all the treasures of wisdom and knowledge; in whom it pleased the Father that all fullness should dwell; *to the end that*, being holy, harmless, undefiled, and full of grace and truth, *he might be thoroughly furnished to execute the office of a mediator*, and surety. Which office he took not unto himself, but was thereunto called by his Father, who put all power and judgment into his hand, and gave him commandment to execute the same" (WCF 8.3, emphasis added). Calvin's comments on a foundational promissory text in this regard, Isa. 11:2, are worth noting, particularly in light of some of the implications I will draw below: "*The Spirit of the Lord*. We must keep in view what I mentioned a little ago, that this refers to Christ's human nature; because he could not be enriched with the gift and grace of the Father, except so far as he became man. Besides, as he came down to us, so he received the gifts of *the Spirit*, that he might bestow them upon us. And this is the *anointing* from which he receives the name of *Christ*, which he imparts to us; for why are we called *Christians*, but because he admits us to his fellowship, by distributing to us out of his fulness *according to the measure* (Eph 4:7) of undeserved liberality? And undoubtedly this passage does not so much as teach us what Christ is in himself, as what he received from the Father, that he might enrich us with his wealth." John Calvin, *Commentary on the Book of the Prophet Isaiah*, trans. William Pringle, vol. 1 (Bellingham, WA: Logos Bible Software, 2010), 374 (emphasis original).

The Spirit of the Lord is upon me,

because he has anointed me

to *proclaim* good news to the poor.

He has sent me to *proclaim* liberty to the captives

and recovering of sight to the blind,

to set at liberty those who are oppressed

to *proclaim* the year of the Lord's favor. (4:18–19)[15]

In Luke's Gospel, Jesus executes his office as Messiah and inaugurates God's promised kingdom under the anointing with the Spirit of the Lord.

In the Old Testament, the Spirit of the Lord came upon individuals to enable them to do what God required them to do. Priests, prophets, and kings were described as in possession of (or possessed by) the Spirit and were said to have been "anointed."[16] The anointing of the Spirit meant that God himself was personally

---

15 Jesus cites Isa. 61:1–2. In chap. 7 we will return to Jesus's sermon in Luke 4 to see the priority it places on preaching in pastoral leadership.

16 The Spirit came upon judges as empowerment to defeat God's enemies and deliver his people (cf. Judg. 3:10; 6:34; 11:29; 13:25; 14:6, 19; 15:14). He came upon individuals to enable them to prophesy (1 Sam. 10:6; 2 Sam. 23:2; 1 Kings 22:24; 2 Chron. 15:1–2; Ezra 1:5) and to give them the revelation necessary for their speech (1 Sam. 10:10; 19:20; Isa. 48:16; 61:1–3). The Spirit also came upon kings to enable them to deliver and rule God's people (Judg. 9:8, 15; 1 Sam. 11:6; 15:17; 16:13; 1 Kings 1:34, 39; 19:15–16; 2 Kings 9:3, 6, 12; 11:12; 23:30; Pss. 45:7–8; 89:20). The language of anointing is used in the consecrating of priests to the service of the Lord (Ex. 28:41; 30:30; 40:15; Lev. 4:3, 5, 16; 6:22; 7:36; 8:11–36; 10:7; Num. 3:3).

According to Geerhardus Vos, over time the very verb "to anoint" acquired the "metaphorical meaning of 'to endow with the Spirit,'" and by the New Testament period, the ideas of anointing and imparting of the Spirit were "entirely self-explanatory." This is particularly the case by the time of Paul's writing, as in 2 Corinthians 1:21, where he refers to believers as being "anointed," which he equates with being "sealed" with the "earnest . . . of the Spirit in our hearts." See Geerhardus Vos, *The Self-Disclosure of*

present and powerfully active in and upon his servants' lives to appoint them to their roles and to empower them with extraordinary ability to fulfill their callings.[17] This prompted Charles Hodge's remarkable statement that when the Spirit anointed individuals, they became "organs of God."[18] To be anointed with the Spirit meant you were God's instrument set apart to serve God's purpose through God's presence and power.

However, "not every impartation of the Spirit" had the same significance.[19] Not everyone was or is the Messiah! As the revelation of redemption progressed, the various aspects of the anointing with the Spirit began to coalesce in the hope of one promised eschatological figure who would be anointed to fulfill, in himself, all of the offices of prophet, priest, and king.[20] This is the back-

---

Jesus: The Modern Debate about the Messianic Consciousness, ed. Johannes Geerhardus Vos (Phillipsburg, NJ: P&R, 1953), 111.

17 The title *the Spirit of the Lord* identifies the third person of the Trinity. Of crucial significance for our study is the fact that, as that divine third person, the Spirit is the person by whom God effects his purposes in the world. Charles Hodge identifies the Spirit of the Lord as "the power or efficiency of God . . . the person through whom the efficiency of God is directly exercised." Charles Hodge, *Systematic Theology*, 3 vols. (Grand Rapids, MI: Eerdmans, 1999), 1:523. Hodge states, "Whatever God does, He does by the Spirit" (529). Further, "The presence of the Spirit is the presence of God" (528), and "the acts of the Spirit are said to be the acts of God" (527).

18 Hodge, *Systematic Theology*, 1:527. Sinclair Ferguson writes that, in the scriptural account, "When the *ruach Yahweh* comes on individuals they are caught up in the thrust of an 'alien' energy and exercise unusual powers. . . . Yahweh's *ruach* is, as it were, the blast of God, the irresistible power by which he accomplishes his purposes, whether creative or destructive." Sinclair B. Ferguson, *The Holy Spirit*, Contours of Christian Theology (Downers Grove, IL: InterVarsity Press, 1996), 17.

19 Vos, *The Self-Disclosure of Jesus*, 110.

20 Vos points to a certain coalescing (of functions at least) of the kingly and priestly offices already in the Old Testament. David danced before the Lord dressed in the linen ephod of the priest (2 Sam. 6:14), and both David and, later, Solomon pronounced the blessing upon the people (2 Sam. 6:18; 1 Kings 8:14). These lines would finally

ground to Jesus's announcement "The Spirit of the Lord is upon me" (Luke 4:18). Luke intends his readers to recognize Jesus as the promised Prophet, Priest, and King, anointed by the Spirit, *the man* with Spirit-given authority and power to establish God's eternal kingdom, particularly through his preaching.

However, while Jesus was *uniquely* anointed to be the Christ, he was that precisely so that he could, at his exaltation, pour out the promised Spirit on all who are his (Luke 3:16; Acts 2:16–21, 38). Geerhardus Vos vividly summarizes the significance of Jesus's baptism with the Spirit for everyone united to him: "The Spirit will rest on the Messiah and the members of His kingdom, passing over from Him to them."[21] To be united to Christ means all that Christ is and did, and all that happened to him, was and is *for* those who believe in him and that believers share with him in it. This is true also of Christ's measureless possession of the Holy Spirit (John 3:34). Every believer in Christ has now received the baptism and is in present possession of the promised Holy Spirit (Acts 2:1–21; Rom. 8:9; 1 Cor. 12:13; 2 Cor. 1:21–22; Eph. 1:11, 13; 1 John 2:20), so that all those who are in Christ now participate in his anointing. For those who are in Christ, the imperative with respect to the Spirit is not to *receive* the Spirit but to be *filled* with the Spirit (Eph. 5:18)—to allow the divine person who has already taken up residence in their lives (1 Cor. 6:19; Gal. 2:20; Eph. 3:16–20; Col. 1:27) to pervade and empower their lives for

---

converge at the arrival of the Messiah himself. See Vos, *The Self-Disclosure of Jesus*, 114.

21 Geerhardus Vos, "The Eschatological Aspect of the Pauline Conception of the Spirit," in *Redemptive History and Biblical Interpretation: The Shorter Writings of Geerhardus Vos*, ed. Richard B. Gaffin Jr. (Phillipsburg, NJ: P&R, 1980), 99.

conformity to Christ (2 Cor. 3:18) and service for Christ (Acts 1:8; 1 Cor. 12:4–11; Eph. 4:7, 12, 16). The question, as it has been put by others, is not *Do we who are in Christ have the Spirit?* but *Does the Spirit really have us?*

What does this have to do with pastoral leadership? The fullness of his Spirit is essential for those whom Christ has appointed to lead in his name. We have seen (chap. 2) that Christ's consummate and infallible abilities to lead, in his office as messianic King, stemmed from his anointing with the Spirit. I have also suggested that this meant a man of God, because he is united to Christ, should mature in his imitation of Christ's leadership competencies. If Christ, the King, executed his ministry by the power of the Spirit, then those who lead united to him are also dependent on his Spirit to extend his ministry. The one upon whom the Spirit rested without measure has poured out his Spirit on his servants to proclaim him from his word in his power. As someone who, in Christ, shares in the anointing of Christ and who is sent by the appointment of Christ, a pastor is God's man set apart and sent by God's Son to preach God's word empowered by God's Spirit. This should cause pastors to consciously cultivate the fullness of the Holy Spirit and to desire, if not expect, the presence and power of the Spirit to be demonstrated in their preaching and leadership.[22] To turn Spurgeon's diagnosis the other way around, this should cause men of God to distinctly recognize and rely on the power of the Holy Spirit for effective ministry.

---

22 A thread woven throughout the Acts of the Apostles is the effect that the presence and power of the Holy Spirit had on the proclamation of Christ through the apostles and others associated with them as his witnesses (Acts 1:8; 2:4, 11, 37, 41; 4:8, 31–33; 6:7–10; 7:54–55; 9:17–21).

Expectations and Aspirations

The preacher-leader should depend on the Spirit for and desire at least three scripturally prescribed effects of the Spirit's power in his stewardship.[23]

First, that his hearers see and respond by faith to *the Christ* who is revealed in the Scriptures and proclaimed through preaching. This is what Paul expected with the Corinthians. The Spirit's power was demonstrated in their believing the word of the cross (1 Cor. 1:17–25), in his illumination and their reception of the wisdom of the revelation that was Paul's gospel (1 Cor. 2:6–13; cf. 1 Thess. 1:5–6).[24] The power of the Spirit in Paul's preaching was demonstrated in that hearers were given ears to hear, eyes to see, and hearts to believe the Christ he proclaimed. As William Still expressed the effect of the Spirit's power in preaching, "Some

23 We may be tempted to think that the effect of the Spirit focuses on the preacher himself, the personal dynamic of his delivery. While a Spirit-filled preacher may indeed be a passionate and dynamic personality, this is not of the essence of the Spirit's power attending preaching. In fact, this seems to have been the misconception behind the Corinthian critique of Paul (2 Cor. 10:10) and directly contrary to the apostle's entire line of defense in 1 Cor. 2:1–3 (cf. 1:17). Paul certainly used words selectively and carefully toward the desired end of presenting a clear, coherent, and compelling message (as time exegeting his letters or analyzing his sermons will demonstrate), but he did not equate the demonstration of the Spirit's power with a particular personality or rhetorical style. Spirit-powered preaching is not *necessarily* tied to the personality and pulpit presence of the preacher. The phenomenon of the Spirit's power in the preacher himself that we are led to expect is his imitating Christ in conformity to his character (1 Cor. 11:1; Phil. 3:17; 1 Tim. 4:12) and his cross (2 Cor. 4:7–12; 12:9–10). See William R. Edwards, "Participants in What We Proclaim: Recovering Paul's Narrative of Pastoral Ministry," *Themelios* 39 no. 3 (2014): 455–69; and Richard B. Gaffin Jr., "The Usefulness of the Cross," *Westminster Theological Journal* 41, no. 2 (1979): 228–46.
24 See Roy E. Ciampa and Brian S. Rosner, *The First Letter to the Corinthians* (Grand Rapids, MI: Eerdmans, 2010), 133; and Richard B. Gaffin Jr., "Some Epistemological Reflections on 1 Cor. 2:6–16," *Westminster Theological Journal* 57, no. 1 (1995): 111–15.

preachers can make people listen to *them*, but the test of a true preacher is whether he can make men listen to *Christ*, and that not with a little temporary interest but with lasting effect." Spirit-empowered preaching "should make men sit up and face Christ."[25] When the Spirit demonstrates his power through preaching, he effects *illumination* in the hearer. A man of God should desire and depend on the Spirit's power so that people would see and believe in Christ.

Second, the Spirit also effects Christlike *transformation* in those he has illumined to believe and receive the word. Paul saw progressive sanctification as a Spirit-given manifestation of the gospel's greater glory in those who had seen and believed Christ (2 Cor. 3:17–18). He was convinced that the word was able to build up the church to sanctification (Acts 20:32) and to effect all the training in righteousness that a man of God was sent to do (2 Tim. 3:16–17; cf. John 17:17). Because the word of God is the sword of the Spirit (Eph. 6:17; cf. Heb. 4:12), when the Spirit demonstrates his power through the reading and preaching of the word, he works in believers to transform their minds and hearts to desire and do (Phil. 2:13; 1 Pet. 1:22–2:2) the will of the Christ revealed in the Scriptures. Pastors should desire and depend on the Spirit's power so that people would grow up into the likeness of Christ.

A third expected effect of Spirit-empowered preaching is *mobilization* in service for Christ. I will dedicate chapter 10 to this topic. But it is important to say here that the gifts that the Spirit has given to believers for the purpose of serving in ministry (Rom. 12:6–8;

---

25 Still, "The Holy Spirit in Preaching," 8–9 (emphasis added).

1 Cor. 12:4–7) are designed to be developed through the proclamation of the word by a man Christ appointed to preach it (Eph. 4:11–16).[26] We can underappreciate the effectiveness of the regular preaching of the word to motivate and mobilize the saints for the stewardship of the gifts Christ has measured out to them. Because it is the Spirit who has given gifts to believers and their use in ministry is dependent upon the Spirit, we should expect that the Spirit would use the preaching of the word he inspired to equip believers for the stewardship he has entrusted to them. For many missionaries and pastors it was the preaching of the word of God that effected the call of God upon their lives. If this is true for calling to ordained office, should we not expect it to be true for equipping the general office to which Christ has called the members of his body?[27] The demonstration of the Spirit's power in preaching effects the mobilization of Christ's body to serve together on Christ's mission. Preacher-leaders should desire and depend on the Spirit's power so that the body of Christ would be mobilized on Christ's mission.

These three effects of the Spirit's power through the preached word could serve as a baseline for a man of God's assessment of his ministry. Rather than being lured by the metrics of worldly success, a pastor could objectively assess the spiritual effectiveness of his leadership by asking the following kinds of questions:

- Are people characteristically helped to see, believe in, and love Christ through my preaching?

26 See chap. 10.

27 See R. B. Kuiper, *The Glorious Body of Christ: A Scriptural Appreciation of the One Holy Church* (Edinburgh: Banner of Truth, 2001), 126–31.

- Are the people I preach to evidencing progress in likeness to Christ?
- Is it characteristic of the body I have been sent to serve that they serve one another, give from what God has given them, and work together in the service of the church's mission?

Again, a discerning assessment might uncover a variety of causes for a seemingly ineffectual ministry, particularly where preaching is indeed textually and doctrinally faithful. However, given all that has been said above, if these effects are not characteristic, a man of God should at least consider whether he is earnestly and intentionally aspiring to and expecting the distinct blessing of the Holy Spirit upon the word preached.

Reasons and Remedies

What should a pastor do if, after discerning assessment, he concludes he has been neglecting or lacking this indispensable spiritual dynamic in his preaching? The answer is found not in following fanciful formulas discovered only by an elite few but in obeying the imperative to be filled with the Spirit (Eph. 5:18). The reality of union with Christ, and all its benefits applied to the pastor and his ministry, means that he should preach and lead as a *Spirit-filled* man of God. The answer for ineffective preaching and leadership is actually found in very ordinary means: a life of communion with the Spirit intentionally applied to the stewardship of pastoral leadership.

The first remedy for powerlessness in pastoral leadership is to *earnestly study God's word*. This might seem redundantly obvious for pastors, but the earnest study of Scripture can become a challenge in the context of pastoral leadership. The loss of vital communion with God in and under his word is a real risk for those whose "job" it is to handle the Scriptures. The Bible can become the textbook or manual of our trade (at which we might be quite skilled craftsmen), but we no longer relate to it as the voice of *my* God *to me*. Yet the Scriptures are the word of the Spirit to the mind and heart of a pastor before they are ever material for his duties. A man of God should not only study the word but readily respond to the word. It is illuminating to notice that, in Paul's theology, the fullness of the Spirit and the rich indwelling of the word of Christ are parallel realities. This is illustrated in the parallel between Ephesians 5:18 and Colossians 3:16:

> And do not get drunk with wine, for that is debauchery, *but be filled with the Spirit*, addressing one another in psalms and hymns and spiritual songs, singing and making melody to the Lord with your heart, giving thanks always and for everything to God the Father in the name of our Lord Jesus Christ. (Eph. 5:18–20)

> Let *the word of Christ dwell in you richly*, teaching and admonishing one another in all wisdom, singing psalms and hymns and spiritual songs, with thankfulness in your hearts to God. (Col. 3:16)

The Scriptures, along with the sacraments and prayer, are a means of grace appointed by the exalted Christ that we may have fellowship with him. For numerous reasons—such as fatigue,

overfamiliarity, discouragement, doubt, overappetite for the plea-
sures of this age—pastors can stop responding to the living God
who relates to them, by his Spirit, through his Scriptures. We must
respond to the word through faith in the promises and purposes
of God, repentance, new obedience, praise, joy, and reforming our
attitudes and actions in our lives and leadership. It's in the context
of this rich indwelling of the word that pastors have communion
with God and are filled with his Spirit.

The second remedy is to *engage in earnest prayer*. Chapter 6 will
focus exclusively on this subject. But we should note here that the
temptation for a preacher (particularly if he has become somewhat competent and confident in his role) is to relegate prayer to
professional and public occasions rather than to approach these
functions through an overflow of habitual private prayer. Prayer
is a God-given means not only for a preacher's own communion
with God but also to express his sincere dependence upon God to
accomplish what his word reveals in those who hear it. Archibald
Alexander stressed to his students that their preaching should be
preceded, accompanied, and followed by much fervent prayer,
even solicited prayers of pious hearers in the congregation:[28]

> As the success of preaching is not owing to the learning or
> eloquence of the organ by which the Word is proclaimed, but
> on the blessing of a sovereign God, we have good ground to
> expect, that in common those ministers who most abound in
> prayer, will see most fruit of their ministry. . . . The preacher of
> the gospel should rise to the pulpit from his knees, and should

---

28 See Garretson, *Princeton and Preaching*, 119.

descend to his knees again from the sacred desk. . . . To study your sermons well is highly important; but to be enabled to pray with sufficient earnestness and importunity is [most] important.[29]

Third, *worship when you are at worship*. Every Christian is called to, and needs to, engage with God in corporate worship every week and in private worship every day. Worship is central to the means of grace God has given to his people for their communion with him. However, pastors can go ages without ever coming to worship *as a worshiper*. Sundays become so busy with managing the worship service that it can be very hard for a pastor to actually engage in the worship he is attempting to lead. The result is that worship, instead of being a God-glorifying, life-giving encounter between a man of God and his God, devolves into a weekly burden in his job description.

A key to the fullness of the Holy Spirit is to worship in Spirit and in truth, and that means that a preacher must not only lead others in worship but also actively worship when the church gathers. This includes the pastor's own participation in the sacraments. It can be all too easy to administer the sacraments to others without fixing one's own faith on the person and promises they signify and seal, by the Spirit, to the recipient by faith. Worshiping while you lead worship means believing, adoring, resting in, and rejoicing in Christ as you administer his means of grace to others.

Fourth, *nurture the relationships God has given you*. Ephesians 4:30 tells us not to grieve the Holy Spirit. This arresting warning

---

29 Alexander, "A Charge Delivered to J. Jones," quoted in Garretson, *Princeton and Preaching*, 120.

comes as Paul describes how relationships are supposed to work between those who are in Christ. We grieve the Spirit (rather than being filled with the Spirit, cf. Eph. 5:18) when we relate to our brothers and sisters in Christ in the un-Christlike ways described in the rest of the chapter (Eph. 4:25–32). In a similar exhortation, Peter tells husbands that their prayers can be hindered if they mistreat their wives (1 Pet. 3:7). God puts a premium on how we relate to other image bearers (Eph. 4:24; James 3:9–10), particularly if they are members of Christ's body, the church.

Preachers can forget or fail to believe how much they actually need the body of Christ for their own care and confrontation. The pace, confidentialities, wounds, and fatigue of pastoral ministry can tempt us toward independence and isolation. The result is that we hear only our own interpretation of things, and lots of wreckage can result, to us and through us, before we recognize it. A pastor may have the luxury of only a few close confidants, but he needs a community of people loving enough and courageous enough to both care for him and confront him. This is for the protection of both the pastor and those he leads. It is not insignificant that the command to be filled with the Spirit appears in the context of some of the most important "one another" exhortations of the New Testament (Eph. 5:18–21). A powerless pulpit could be the result of the preacher neglecting relationships God has called him to nurture, or of contenting himself with fractured and broken relationships, thus grieving the Holy Spirit (Eph. 4:30). In the next chapter we'll see how the fullness of the Spirit is evidenced in the man of God's example, in his manners and mode, with and for the people of God.

Conclusion

Thomas Goodwin began his treatise on the Holy Spirit with concern about neglect of conscious communion with him. Goodwin wrote:

> There is a general omission in the saints of God, in their not giving the Holy Ghost that glory that is due to his person, and for his great work of salvation in us, insomuch that *we have in our hearts almost lost this third person.* We give daily in our thoughts, prayers, affections, and speeches, an honour to the Father and the Son; but who almost directs the aims of his praise . . . unto God the Holy Ghost? He is a person in the Godhead equal with the Father and the Son; and the work he doth for us in its kind is as great as those of the Father or the Son. Therefore, by the equity of all law, a proportionable honour from us is due to him.[30]

In our day, often legitimate reactions to errors and excesses in particular theological and pastoral traditions can deaden a pastor's heart toward any aspiration for or expectation of the Spirit's power in the pastor's stewardship. It is possible to confess and contend for a formally correct doctrine of the Spirit while functionally neglecting conscious, personal fellowship with the Spirit of that doctrine. As someone once put it, the "already, not-yet" of what Christ has done can easily be diluted to "already, not-much" in our aspirations for what he can do.

---

30 Thomas Goodwin, *The Works of Thomas Goodwin*, vol. 6, *The Work of the Holy Ghost in Our Salvation* (Edinburgh: James Nichol, 1863), 3 (emphasis added).

The goal of this chapter has been to equip men of God to distinctly recognize and rely on the power of the Holy Spirit for effective pastoral leadership. The presence and power of the Spirit is not something God is unwilling to provide. Jesus assured his disciples of the Father's willingness in Luke 11:13: "If you then, who are evil, know how to give good gifts to your children, how much more will the heavenly Father give the Holy Spirit to those who ask him!" The Father has willingly given the Spirit to all who have faith in the Son. Should we now doubt that he is willing to supply fullness and power for the stewardship to which he has appointed us?

Spirit-empowered preaching and leadership comes through a Spirit-filled man of God, one who walks in communion with God before he ever walks to the pulpit to speak for God. Thus Charles Hodge wrote of his professor and mentor Archibald Alexander that "the great secret of his power" was his "habitual fellowship with God."[31] Pastoral leadership that demonstrates the Spirit's power and, therefore, leads individuals and congregations into God's purposes overflows from the heart of a man of God who is consciously cultivating communion with God, in Christ, by the Spirit.

---

31 Charles Hodge, "*The Life of Archibald Alexander,* a Review," in James M. Garretson, *Pastor-Teachers of Old Princeton: Memorial Addresses for the Faculty of Princeton Theological Seminary, 1812–1921* (Edinburgh: Banner of Truth, 2012), 45.

Set the believers an example in speech, in conduct, in love, in faith, in purity.

1 TIMOTHY 4:12

5

The Example of a Man of God

Christlike Character

WHILE THIS BOOK was being written, the church was rocked again and again by dramatic and devastating news of corrupt pastoral leaders. One popular preacher-leader abandoned his faith and his marriage. A respected apologist was discovered to have lived a secret life of immorality, financial corruption, and wicked manipulation of those who had trusted him for spiritual care. A pastor who had reached the heights of celebrity was dethroned from his ministry empire because of angry, unaccountable, brutal leadership of colleagues and blatant dishonesty for financial gain. Denominational leaders were being investigated and called to account for covering up vile sins perpetrated by false shepherds.

These are merely a sampling of the cases of corrupted character and their ruinous consequences exposed publicly. By the time wickedness like these examples makes headlines, there have typically been repeated episodes of less known compromises in the offending leader's life, incremental concessions that C. S. Lewis called "those little marks or twists on the central inside part of the soul which are going to turn it, in the long run, into . . . a hellish creature."[1] The most scandalous hypocrisies are often rooted in seemingly less significant character issues that have gone unaddressed in the life of a pastor. One person whose double life was exposed told me: "My life was like a series of separate little boxes I kept in a mental closet. Each one was filled with a different identity for who I would be in different roles and with different people. I had to be careful there was no crossover of the boxes." His strategy for secret sin was to compartmentalize his identity, disintegrate who he was.

Because pastoral leadership is the process where a man of God leads the people of God by preaching the word of God, the pastor's example is essential to the process of leadership. The walk of a man of God must be integrated with the word he has been sent to preach. He must pursue conformity to Christ as he leads for Christ, because his stewardship includes the duty to serve as an example for those to whom he preaches (1 Tim. 4:12; cf. Titus 2:7; 1 Pet. 5:3).

Paul stressed the need for deliberate and disciplined integration of manner and message in pastoral leadership. In both of his letters to Timothy he exhorted him to be intentional, energetic, and uncompromising in making personal progress toward character that conformed to the Master he represented (1 Tim. 4:7–12; 6:11; 2 Tim. 2:20–23). Timothy was to actively avoid certain behaviors (1 Tim. 4:7; 6:4; cf. 3:3; 2 Tim. 2:16, 23–26)

---

1 C. S. Lewis, *Mere Christianity* (New York: Macmillan, 1960), 92.

and affections (1 Tim. 6:11; cf. 3:3; 6:6–10; 2 Tim. 2:22) and to energetically pursue conformity to the righteousness of the Christ whose righteousness was his already by faith. When these exhortations are addressed in popular messages, the emphasis often boils down to "don't ruin your life and your ministry." This is indeed an important emphasis and an understandable reaction to the wreckage that results from neglecting them. But when we read Paul's exhortations as solely, or perhaps primarily, about the preacher's personal holiness, we can dilute the full motivation to pursue Christlike leadership. The apostle's exhortations to Timothy were not merely for the protection of his holiness as a personal matter (as crucial as that is). Paul exhorted Timothy *so that*, as a steward of God's house, he could be useful to his Master (2 Tim. 2:21) and could serve as his example to his people. Timothy's conduct was to witness to the content of his preaching.

The Type of His Example

The word translated "example" in 1 Timothy 4:12 was used to refer to the pattern for the impress on a signet ring, or a die for the image on a coin, or a sculpture. It implies a mold or model for making an impression or image that *typifies* something or someone.[2] The apostle used it elsewhere to refer to his role as an

---

2   See "Τύπος," in *Exegetical Dictionary of the New Testament*, ed. Horst Robert Balz and Gerhard Schneider, vol. 3 (Grand Rapids, MI: Eerdmans, 1990), 37; Frederick W. Danker, Walter Bauer, William F. Arndt, and F. Wilbur Gingrich, *A Greek-English Lexicon of the New Testament and Other Early Christian Literature*, 3rd ed. (Chicago: University of Chicago Press, 2000), 1019–20; and Leonhard Goppelt, "Τύπος, Ἀντίτυπος, Τυπικός, Ὑποτύπωσις," in *Theological Dictionary of the New Testament*, ed. Gerhard Kittel and Gerhard Friedrich, trans. Geoffrey W. Bromiley, vol. 8 (Grand Rapids, MI: Eerdmans, 1964), 246–49.

example of Christ to others and to call the church to imitate him and those who walked in his pattern (Phil. 3:17; 2 Thess. 3:9; 1 Tim. 1:16; 2 Tim. 1:13; cf. 1 Cor. 11:1). So, when Timothy, who had followed his mentor's footsteps (2 Tim. 3:10), read the imperative to be an example for believers, he would have understood that his conduct was to leave an impression that represented his message. He was to image Christ for those to whom he preached Christ.[3] This is why the disintegration of doctrine and life in a pastor is not merely a personal problem. It maligns his character and hinders his usefulness to the one who sent him to speak in his name. Because a man of God is the sent servant of Christ the King, he must represent his Master not only in the message he bears but also in his manner of life and leadership.

The Motive for His Example

This exemplary aspect should fuel motivation for character in pastoral leadership. We must be motivated by nothing less than love, both for the Christ we exemplify and for those he has sent us to lead to him in our pursuit of conformity to Christ. For Paul, love held priority among the fruit to be pursued and produced in the Christian life (1 Cor. 13:13; Gal. 5:22). Love is the mode by which believers are to imitate God's character (godliness) toward one another (Eph. 5:1–2).[4] Love is the motive from which the

---

3   "Appointment to leadership must be accompanied by a moral life which will act as a refutation of heretical leaders. Timothy can be a 'type' to others because he himself is moulded by the gospel." I. Howard Marshall and Philip H. Towner, *A Critical and Exegetical Commentary on the Pastoral Epistles*, International Critical Commentary (London: T&T Clark, 2004), 561.

4   For a pastorally penetrating exposition of how the believer's love toward others is to image God's love, see John Murray, *Principles of Conduct: Aspects of Biblical Ethics* (Grand Rapids, MI: Eerdmans, 1957), 177–78.

stewardship of ministry gifts should flow (Rom. 12:8–9; Eph. 4:2, 16). Without love all the gifts, activities, and attainments in any ministry (by church leaders or members) is useless (1 Cor. 13:1–3).[5] Love is central to the virtues Timothy was to pursue (1 Tim. 6:11), and love was integral to the endowment of the Spirit to Timothy for his stewardship (2 Tim. 1:7). Love was a hallmark of the example Paul himself had set for Timothy (2 Tim. 3:10). Love was the motive that Paul pressed on Timothy at the outset of his letter (1 Tim. 1:5), and love was to be a primary mark of Timothy's own example (1 Tim. 4:12). Love is the motivational root and primary fruit of pastoral leadership that imitates Christ to his people.[6] As Archibald Alexander put it in a lecture to his students on the nature of the pastor's office:

The love of Christ . . . should suggest all his plans, guide all his operations, give energy to all his efforts, and afford him comfort under all his trials. . . . This holy affection should impel him to undertake the most arduous duties, and encounter the most formidable dangers; this should enkindle the ardour of his eloquence, and supply the pathos of his most tender addresses. . . . *Nothing but the love of Christ can make a truly faithful pastor*, or evangelist, assiduous in all his services, and indefatigable in the most private and self-denying duties of his office. Other motives

5 "Without love . . . the purpose of the gifts of the Spirit is thwarted." Sinclair B. Ferguson, *The Holy Spirit*, Contours of Christian Theology (Downers Grove, IL: InterVarsity Press, 1996), 209.

6 "The fulfilment of the law springs from love to God and our fellowmen. And this must mean that the practice of the biblical *ethos*, the bringing to expression and fruition of the behaviour required and approved by the biblical revelation, springs from this love." Murray, *Principles of Conduct*, 21.

may lead a man to great diligence in preparing for his labours in the pulpit. . . . Other motives may stimulate a minister to great public exertion . . . but if supreme love to Christ be wanting, he is, after all, nothing; or, at best, a mere "sounding brass or tinkling cymbal." Genius, learning, eloquence, zeal, public exertion, and great sacrifices, even if it should be all of our goods, and our lives themselves, will be accounted of no value, in the eyes of the Lord, if love to Christ be wanting.[7]

This needs to be emphasized for at least two reasons. First, I have stressed the need for the power of the Spirit in a man of God's stewardship, and the primary consequence of the Spirit's empowering presence is love. It is the first "fruit" of the Spirit's fullness not merely in order of the text (Gal. 5:22) but also in the priorities of the Spirit's work. Love is the Spirit's "deepest and most proper work."[8] The most basic and lasting transformation by the power of the Holy Spirit that ought to be seen in a man of God is love for God's commands and God's people.[9] The love a preacher must have for and demonstrate to others is not simply a natural affection produced by personal affinity in relationship, innate personality, or professionally developed people skills.

---

7   A. A. Alexander, "The Pastoral Office," quoted in James M. Garretson, *Princeton and Preaching* (Carlisle, PA: Banner of Truth, 2005), 127 (emphasis added).

8   Abraham Kuyper, *The Work of the Holy Spirit* (New York: Funk & Wagnalls, 1900), 508.

9   Cf. 1 Cor. 13:8, 13. Abraham Kuyper emphasized the priority of Spirit-produced love this way: "And this is the proper work of the Holy Spirit, that shall remain His forevermore. When there remains no more sin to be atoned for, nor any unholiness to be sanctified, when all the elect shall jubilate before the throne, even then the Holy Spirit shall perform this divine work of keeping the Love of God actively dwelling in their hearts." Kuyper, *The Work of the Holy Spirit*, 520.

Plenty of pastors love those who love them, and they are savvy enough to be gracious in social situations. A Christ-imitating preacher-leader loves sinners! He loves sufferers who need seemingly unending investment of his resources. He loves those who are slow to learn or hard-heartedly resist what is preached. He loves those who hurt him and those who treat him like their enemy. Christ-exemplifying love is the primary transformative effect and character trait of the Spirit's power in a man of God.

The second reason love needs to be emphasized is that we can easily miss the root cause of immorality and other publicly scandalous sins of character. As we will see below, Paul emphasizes other inseparable fruits of Christlikeness characteristic of a man of God in the Pastorals (e.g., 1 Tim. 4:12). Not least are the tested character qualifications for office listed in 1 Timothy 3:1–13 and Titus 1:6–9. These have received necessary and excellent exposition elsewhere.[10] But it is love, toward both God and others (Matt. 22:37–39) that draws a man of God toward godly character and conduct with the people he leads. And it is love that drives him away from attitudes and actions that could harm others and the reputation of Christ. Without love, the preacher-leader will not desire the standard of Christ-conformity he is called to, far less exemplify it.[11] In other words, it is important to realize that leaders who are exposed in headline-worthy scandals have a love problem

10 For example, see Jonathan Gibson's recent excellent treatment of 1 Tim. 3:1–7 in "Orthopraxy: The Life of the Minister in the Life of His Ministry" (forthcoming). Viewable on YouTube at https://www.youtube.com/watch?v=ZMCrC76wdtA.

11 Murray emphasizes the role of love in living to the standard God sets for us: "It is impossible for the prescriptions of law to have scope in our relationships to our fellow-men *unless love reigns supreme*, love as both expulsive and impulsive affection, expulsive of evil and impulsive to good." Murray, *Principles of Conduct*, 22 (emphasis added).

long before they have a sex or money problem. Love must be the animating affection for the pastor's leadership ethic.

However, Spirit-empowered love is not merely an affection; it bears fruit in action.[12] John Murray describes the biblical concept of love as "both emotive and motive; love is feeling and it impels to action."[13] This is why Paul makes the expressions of godliness sprinkled through the Pastorals so concrete and gives such objective definition to the fruit of love in places like 1 Corinthians 13:4–7. A paraphrase of that familiar passage can help to objectify what Christ-exemplifying love looks like in a pastoral leader:

> The loving leader is patient and kind; the loving leader does not envy or boast; the loving leader is not arrogant or rude. The loving leader does not insist on his own way; the loving leader is not irritable or resentful; the loving leader does not rejoice at wrongdoing, but rejoices with the truth. The loving leader bears all things; the loving leader believes all things; the loving leader hopes all things; the loving leader endures all things. (see 1 Cor. 13:1–7; cf. 2 Tim. 2:24–26)

Love, biblically defined, not only desires—it *does* the right thing, and *does not do* the wrong!

---

12 See, for example, the active expressions of love for God and neighbor (Matt. 22:37–39) commanded in the Decalogue (Ex. 20:1–19), in the Sermon on the Mount (Matt. 5:21–6:4), and by Paul (Rom. 13:8–10; Gal. 5:13–23). Murray stresses, "It is not otiose emotion but love as both emotive and motive, intensely preoccupied with him who is its supreme object, and therefore intensely active in the doing of his will." Murray, *Principles of Conduct*, 23.

13 Murray, *Principles of Conduct*, 22.

The Manner of His Example

Love as affection in action has at least three implications for a man of God who seeks to exemplify Christ. He must be a *sanctified* leader, a *servant* leader, and a *stalwart* leader.

Sanctified Leadership

Because the man of God has been united to Christ before he is appointed by him, he is, first and fundamentally, a son of God before he is a steward of the mysteries of God. That means he has received the grace not only of the imputed righteousness of Christ but also of the Spirit dwelling within him to conform him to the image of Christ.[14] This is why Paul could use very active and energetic language to describe Timothy's duty to discipline himself toward personal holiness and away from ungodliness (1 Tim. 4:7; 6:11; 2 Tim. 2:22). Sadly, there is a brand of "gospel-centered" preaching and pastoring that celebrates an unwary attitude toward the dangers of spiritual warfare and exemplifies an antinomian disposition toward Scripture's demands of righteous living. According to this brand of love, some contemporary preacher-leaders are more compelled to decry what they pejoratively label "purity culture" than they are concerned to model the maxim often attributed to Robert Murray M'Cheyne, "The greatest need of my people is my personal holiness."[15] But the love of God that the man of God

---

14 See chaps. 2 and 4.

15 Though widely attributed to M'Cheyne, the statement is difficult to document and appears to be "oral tradition." I take the sentiment behind the statement to express the reality behind 1 Tim. 4:12, 16—that people needed the pastor's example of Christ to go with his teaching of Christ, not that M'Cheyne's (or any other pastor's) holiness was in some way efficacious for his congregation.

is to exemplify is "a *holy* Love, intolerant of evil."[16] And this holy intolerance must be focused first on his own character and conduct. Precisely because love fulfills the law (Rom. 13:8–10; Gal. 5:14), the man in whose heart the love of God has been poured out (Rom. 5:5) increasingly desires and disciplines himself to be conformed to God's will, revealed in his word (Rom. 6:1–8, 17, 19)—particularly when he is a messenger of that word! This applies not only to the fruit of action but also to the root affections that produce those actions (Ps. 119:97; Prov. 4:23; Matt. 5:21–22, 28; Luke 6:45). After all, while love is not *merely* an affection, it *is* affection, and loving God with our whole persons (Matt. 22:37) means setting the desires of our hearts on what he prescribes and not on what he prohibits. Holy love loves the holiness of God. And a man of God, who desires to lead God's people to maturity in godliness, disciplines himself in his own pursuit of holiness in order to exemplify it to others.[17]

This has deep implications for pastoral leadership. Along with the typical (and necessary) exhortations on how preachers should guard their hearts and walk regarding the temptations that lead to headline-making sins, sanctified leadership is also about how a man of God listens to others, speaks, argues, and responds to loss and disappointment. The temptations that accompany leadership responsibility in terms of integrity of speech, personal ambition, jealousy, anger, bitterness, or greed are also all oppor-

---

16 Kuyper, *The Work of the Holy Spirit*, 514–15.

17 The point here is not to expound the entire doctrine of sanctification in Christ but to argue that, in order to be the spokesman and example for Christ he has been sent to be, the man of God must diligently apply the doctrine and duties of sanctification to his own life.

tunities to image Christ's character to his people. A man of God must be intentional in exemplifying the likeness of Christ from the heart in the conversations, relational tensions, opportunities for personal gain, and allurements of sensuality and immorality that troll pastors.

Servant Leadership

Abraham Kuyper was a preacher-leader, a pastor who also led a nation.[18] Kuyper's works include a noteworthy book on the Holy Spirit in which he describes the love produced by the Spirit as always imaging the cross. He wrote, "Since this love attained its severest tension on Calvary, its symbol is and ever shall be the Cross."[19] Love that is the fruit of the Spirit will be cross-shaped.

Paul intentionally exemplified a cross-shaped model of leadership to Timothy (2 Tim. 3:11), and he described his reason for adopting this pattern to the church in Corinth (1 Cor. 1:17–25).[20] His preaching and leadership had been opposed there, because the Corinthians thought of glory according to the "wisdom" of their culture. To a Corinthian, wisdom was the ability to present yourself as powerful and polished and thereby win the crowd and gain glory. Glory was seen as the success, status, wealth, and honor afforded by the community and culture in this age. This

18 Kuyper served as prime minister of the Netherlands 1901–1905.

19 Kuyper, *The Work of the Holy Spirit*, 519.

20 A portion of this section first appeared in my "The Manner and the Message: 1 Corinthians 2:4," *TableTalk*, August 2019, 14–15; https://tabletalkmagazine.com/article/2019/08/1-corinthians-24/. For the cultural background of what follows, see Duane Litfin, *St. Paul's Theology of Proclamation: 1 Corinthians 1–4 and Greco-Roman Rhetoric* (New York: Cambridge University Press, 1994); and Anthony C. Thiselton, *The First Epistle to the Corinthians*, The New International Greek Testament Commentary (Grand Rapids, MI: Eerdmans, 2000), 12–16.

philosophy was exemplified by traveling orators, called sophists. Classical philosophers had sought to put words well in the service of truth, beauty, and the public good, but sophists were essentially merchants of spin. They adopted the forms of skillful oratory to create an image of great thought and bearing for the purpose of self-promotion. Image, not substance, was the point of their speech. Paul's rhetoric and personal presence did not impress crowds like these popular sophists. Conformed to the culture as they were, the Corinthian church saw the apostle as weak and doubted that he was the leader best suited to serve their interests (cf. 2 Cor. 10:10; 12:9–10).[21]

Leaders and pastors who face the kinds of criticisms Paul did can be tempted to respond in wrong ways. One response is to become *authoritarian*: to assert yourself and your will for your interests, regardless of the costs to others. Another temptation is to *accommodate*: to repackage and redefine your message and manner according to the wisdom of the culture in order to succeed or survive. A third response is to *abdicate*: to distort the biblical ideas of humility, gentleness, and servant leadership into an excuse to avoid responsibility to define and defend the church's beliefs, set direction, and make decisions. The criticism and conflicts inherent in pastoral leadership can tempt a man of God to default to a manner in leadership contrary to the character and wisdom of Christ.

---

21 Exhibit A is the division of loyalties—some following Paul; some, Apollos; some, Cephas—referred to in 1 Cor. 1:12, which is almost certainly a matter of preferred style rather than doctrinal distinction. Paul would hardly have shied from confronting a brother in Christ on a doctrinal matter that was dividing the church, even Peter (cf. Gal. 2:11), and would certainly not have aligned his labors so closely with Apollos (1 Cor. 3:5–8) had they been divided doctrinally.

Paul didn't take the bait. He explained that his message about Christ compelled him to imitate and exemplify the manner of Christ, who was the self-sacrificing servant (1 Cor. 1:17).[22] For Christ's apostle to adopt postures that his critics thought more culturally plausible would have betrayed his message, evincing a lack of integrity between his word and his walk (cf. 1 Tim. 4:16). Paul's theology shaped his leadership biography, and that meant his leadership manner had to be intentionally cross-shaped. And when he later wrote, "Be imitators of me, as I am of Christ" (1 Cor. 11:1), he made it explicit that he was not merely recording his biography but also exemplifying a pattern for others to follow.

Men of God who would exemplify the Christ of the message they proclaim must adopt a pattern of cross-shaped servant leadership. This means intentionally calibrating our manner of leadership to contrast with a culture of self-promotion, because we are spokesmen of the self-humbling Savior who said, "For even the Son of Man came not to be served but to serve, and to give his life as a ransom for many" (Mark 10:45). It means, in humility, counting others

22 When he wrote that Christ sent him to preach the gospel "*and not with words of eloquent wisdom*, lest the cross of Christ be emptied of its power" (1:17), he emphasized his intentional choice not to be like sophists. Joel Beeke warns against a misapplication of Paul's statement: "Let us not twist these phrases into a rejection of all human intelligence and rational argument. . . . His writings are not rambling streams of consciousness." Joel Beeke, "Plain Preaching: Demonstrating the Spirit and His Power," *Reformed Presbyterian Theological Journal* 5, no. 1 (2018): 9. Paul did not disavow the need to choose words well and argue clearly and persuasively in preaching or leadership. Nor did he doubt the efficacy of the cross to accomplish all that God had ordained. First Corinthians 1:18–31 explains what he meant. The logic of the argument is supplied by the preposition "for" at the beginning of verse 18. This section, which reveals a glorious theology of the cross, is actually a supporting argument for what he has asserted in verse 17.

as more significant than ourselves and looking out not only for our interests but also for the interests of others, while avoiding selfish ambition and conceit (Phil. 2:1–8).[23] This turns pastoral leadership upside down (or right side up) from the dominant leadership culture of this age.

It is striking to notice how Paul describes those who, in the last days, "have the appearance of godliness" but deny its power (2 Tim. 3:1–5). These religious hypocrites are driven and defined also by love. They love self, money, pleasure; and according to the vices highlighted in the passage, they use and abuse others in their own self-interest rather than giving themselves for the good of others. This could be a searching diagnostic for some in pastoral leadership. When your manner proclaims, "*You* lay down your life for *me*" rather than "I desire and do what is for your eternal good in Christ, even if it costs me my life," you are leading like a Gentile and not like Christ (Luke 22:24–27; Eph. 5:25–27). A man of God is called to exemplify willing service for the eternal best interests of those who are yet in the snare of the devil (2 Tim. 2:24–26; cf. Rom. 5:8), not to self-promotion, self-preservation, and self-protection. This means (at least) resisting the temptation, even in the face of personal opposition, to assert self-interest and authoritarianism in the stewardship of pastoral leadership.[24] Christ-exemplifying, loving leadership is self-sacrificing servant leadership.

---

23 "There is a certain accent which keeps recurring in the passages on imitation. It is the accent of humility, self-denial, self-giving, self-sacrifice for the sake of Christ and the salvation of others." Willis Peter De Boer, *The Imitation of Paul: An Exegetical Study* (Kampen: Free University of Amsterdam, 1962), 207.

24 Cf. Eph. 6:4, 9 and the exposition of the commands to superiors in the Westminster Larger Catechism 129–30.

Stalwart Leadership

But servant leadership is not *non*leadership! The biblical concept of servant leadership is sometimes perverted as an excuse to abdicate the responsibility entrusted to pastors. Superficial sentiment labeled as love can mask convictional cowardice and deflect a pastor's responsibility to declare and defend biblical teaching, set biblical direction, and make biblical decisions for the sake of God's people. Fear of the costs of faithful leadership leads to accommodation of falsehood, error, or corruption under the guise of "servant leadership." Such fecklessness was not what Paul understood by exemplary, Christlike love or servant leadership.

Precisely because Paul was a servant under orders from his Lord and embraced the cost of that commission (Acts 20:24), he confronted the idolatries and immoralities of the age and in the church. Some of the most loving, grace-soaked words in the Scriptures, "And such were some of you" (1 Cor. 6:11), appear in the very context where Paul uncompromisingly warns against the immorality-fostering ideologies by which the church can be deceived (1 Cor. 6:9). At the end of the very letter that he began by describing his cross-shaped manner of leadership, Paul exhorts God's people using biblically militant and masculine language: "Be watchful, stand firm in the faith, act like men, be strong. Let all that you do be done in love" (1 Cor. 16:13–14).

The apostle certainly did not see love and truth as antithetical concerns when he exhorted Timothy to "charge certain persons not to teach any different doctrine" (1 Tim. 1:3), to "wage the good warfare" (1:18), and to "command and teach" the things that accorded with sound doctrine and correct the false (1 Tim. 4:11;

cf. 4:6). Paul used militant language to charge him to "fight the good fight" (1 Tim. 6:12) and to "guard the deposit" (1 Tim. 6:20; 2 Tim. 1:14) as "a good soldier" (2 Tim. 2:2–3). Timothy was accountable, as the Lord's servant, to rightly handle the word of truth (2 Tim. 2:15) and correct opponents as he preached the word of God, which included the ministry of reproof and rebuke contra the personal passions and trends of the time (2 Tim. 4:1–4).

A portrait of Christ the King, as he is promised in the Psalms, helps us to see this aspect of his character that the preacher-leader should imitate:

> You are the most handsome of the sons of men;
>> *grace* is poured upon your lips;
>> therefore God has blessed you forever.
> Gird your sword on your thigh, O mighty one,
>> In your splendor and majesty!
>
> In your majesty ride out victoriously
>> for the cause of *truth and meekness and righteousness*;
>> let your right hand teach you awesome deeds!
> Your arrows are sharp
>> in the heart of the king's enemies;
>> the peoples fall under you. (Ps. 45:2–5)

Christ the King is perfectly proportioned in meekness and awesome militant majesty. This is the Christ who has sent a man of God and to whom that man is united. Therefore, Christ-exemplifying leadership is not amorphous, a-doctrinal sentimentality that abdicates responsibility for conviction, confrontation, and correction. In fact, the opposite is true. Love for God's glory and for the good of God's people compels a man of God to give his life in order to be clear and courageous in the proclamation and protection of the word entrusted to him.

In 1944 Professor John Murray gave a greeting to the incoming class of pastors in training at Westminster Theological Seminary. The convocation occurred just three weeks after D-Day, and many of the incoming students' peers were giving their lives for the great cause in Europe. Murray seized the leadership moment and charged the students with appropriately militant language:

> You have come here, we trust, because of divine compulsion. . . . You are under the compulsion of a divine call to the greatest vocation upon earth. . . . In a very peculiar and pre-eminent sense you are here as good soldiers of Jesus Christ, and as such you are performing the highest service to God, and to Caesar. You are performing, even to your country, to the United Nations, yes, to the world, the highest ministry that can be rendered. For you are preparing yourselves in pursuance of a divine call for the ministry of the Word without which the whole world perishes in sin, in misery and death. You are training for the most militant service in that kingdom which is an everlasting kingdom and in that dominion which shall not be destroyed.[25]

In this age Christ's mission requires Christ's servants to remain stalwart for his truth, without which those who yet resist his truth will perish in their sin. Fighting the good fight, and the

25 John Murray, *Collected Writings of John Murray*, vol. 1, *The Claims of Truth* (Edinburgh: Banner of Truth, 1976), 105.

self-sacrifice it requires, is an expression of exemplary, Christlike, Spirit-produced love in pastoral leadership.

Conclusion

Being an example is essential in the process of pastoral leadership. It is essential not just because an example has the power to inspire followers but also because it has the potential in Christ's appointed leaders to point God's people to his purposes for them in Christ. Therefore, integrity between the pastor's walk and the word he proclaims is crucial. Before you turn to the next chapter, take some time to look in the mirror and ask (Ps. 139:23–24) if there is any disconnect in your life or leadership that could distract God's people from following God's purposes for them. Ask trusted counselors if they see any ways in which you could not say to those entrusted to your leadership, "Follow me, as I follow Christ." Then take any disintegration you see to Christ, who has given himself *for you* and lives *in you* (Gal. 2:20); ask for his Spirit to empower your imitation of him for the good of those you seek to lead for him.

That's where the leader of Christ's mission to the Gentiles went for power to lead God's people. While he sought to set an example to follow, he did not depend on his example to accomplish the King's purposes. He depended on the King himself and asked him to work in his power, through prayer. That's where the process of pastoral leadership will take us next—to the practice of leading through prayer!

PART 2

PRACTICES

To study your sermons well is highly important;
but to be enabled to pray with sufficient earnestness
and importunity is [most] important.

A. A. ALEXANDER

I believe that no man can have any evidence
in his own soul that he doth conscientiously
perform any ministerial duty toward his flock,
who doth not continually pray for them.

JOHN OWEN

6

The Posture of a Man of God

Leading from Your Knees

JEREMIAH LANPHIER was a businessman who served as a missionary to New York's Lower East Side. He was earnest in door-to-door evangelism and tract distribution, and as he made his evangelistic rounds each day, he would pray regularly, "Lord, what wilt thou have me to do?"[1] Lanphier decided to begin a noon-hour prayer meeting once a week for businessmen. One noon hour in the fall of 1857 he opened the upper lecture hall at Old Dutch Church on Fulton Street and knelt to pray—alone. Thirty minutes later he heard footsteps on the stairs and was joined by others. The number grew to six. Over the next four weeks attendance at the prayer meeting grew incrementally until, by mid-October 1857, one hundred people (including unbelievers experiencing conviction of sin) came every day to the church for prayer.

---

1 Samuel I. Prime, *The Power of Prayer* (Edinburgh: Banner of Truth, 1991), 5.

Noon-hour prayer meetings spread around the city in churches, fire houses, police stations, stores, and a theater. One newspaper was compelled to call the noon hour in New York the hour of prayer![2] The movement spread beyond New York throughout the nation, effecting a widespread work of God that resulted in the conversion and moral reformation of multitudes. It came to be known as the revival of 1857–1860.

I recall hearing a respected Scottish preacher reminisce about a prayer meeting started in Scotland in the middle of the twentieth century. A couple of ruling elders in the Church of Scotland covenanted to meet together every week to pray for revival in their church. The sad state of the Church of Scotland today might cause one to question what effect their prayers had. But in the latter part of the twentieth century the Church of Scotland was served by some great evangelical pastors. As the story is told, the weekly prayer meeting never grew beyond those two elders, and after a couple of years of weekly meetings, their burden lifted and the prayer meeting disbanded—without any observable signs in answer to their prayers. However, some years later, it was calculated that many of those great evangelical pastors in the church were called and trained for the ministry during the period those elders were praying.[3]

Early in my ministry God granted me the blessing of seeing the transformative effect of concerted prayer. I served as a youth pastor in a church that had experienced dramatic decline due to

---

2   Iain H. Murray, *Revival and Revivalism: The Making and Marring of American Evangelicalism, 1750–1858* (Edinburgh: Banner of Truth, 1994), 343.

3   I recall hearing this story at a conference at College Church, Wheaton, IL, in 1994 and have since confirmed the sources contemporary to the movement.

an economic crisis in the community. The church's youth group had once been known throughout the denomination for its discipleship of young people, many of whom became pastors and missionaries. In the first weeks of my ministry there the youth group consisted of three to five young people attending a weekly event. In desperate dependence on God, we initiated a weekly prayer gathering for youth leaders and the young people.

The prayer group developed a list of names of unbelieving friends they desired to expose to the gospel. The gathering grew in numbers, and young people on the list of unbelievers also began to attend the prayer meeting. A couple of them came to faith through the prayer group. God's blessing on the preaching of the word at weekly gatherings and evangelistic events became evident. When God called me to another pastorate several years later, disciples were multiplying and maturing significantly in the youth group. The spiritual fruit was beyond what we could have asked for or imagined, and I'm convinced the soil was cultivated in that weekly prayer meeting.

The history of the church is stitched through with examples of God using his people's prayers to extend Christ's kingdom and mission in the world. That history testifies to a scriptural pattern that forms the first of our practices in pastoral leadership. The church is led to maturity on her mission through intentional, earnest, persistent intercessory prayer. A man of God leads *from his knees*!

The Apostolic Pattern

The apostles both practiced and prescribed leadership through intentional, earnest, persistent intercessory prayer. And they learned it from Jesus. Ephesians 3:14–21 is one conspicuous example of how the apostles understood prayer to work in the leadership of the church. Paul's prayer in chapter 3 serves as the pivot from precept to practice in his leadership of the mission at Ephesus. In the first two chapters of Ephesians the apostle discloses what God has done for his people, solely by grace. In the last three chapters he emphasizes how the church must now live in that grace. Ephesians 3:10 discloses the glorious end goal of the church, which should serve as the great motivation of a man of God as he leads God's people on Christ's mission: that through the church's growth in maturity, God's manifold glory might be cosmically displayed. It is with that inspired vision in the immediate rear view that Paul prays as he does in 3:14–21, and as he is about to tell the church how to live in order to realize that vision (Eph. 4–6). Paul makes the pivot from precept to practice in the life and mission of the church through prayer.

This is deeply significant for pastoral leadership in Christ's church. The apostle is very purposeful in what he is doing; notice his words "for this reason" (Eph. 3:14). He has just proclaimed the gospel to the Ephesians and is aware of what he is about to call them to do, as those who, in Christ, have received "every spiritual blessing in the heavenly places" (Eph. 1:3), so he bows his knees before the Father. A full exposition of the prayer would show that the goal of the prayer is expressed in verse 19: that the believers might be "filled with all the fullness of God." That essentially means "you would grow to full maturity in the character of God in the likeness of Christ." Paul is praying for nothing less than the very purpose of God for the life of the church in Christ, that as Christians worship, work, and walk together, they would be conformed to the character of Christ for the glory of God (cf. Rom. 8:29; Eph. 1:6; 3:10; 4:13, 15). In other words, the apostle has delivered the propositions about what is true of them in Christ, and he wants them to grow into the fullness of what God has purposed for them in Christ. *For this reason*, he adopts the posture of prayer. The leader of Christ's mission among the Gentiles is leading from his knees.

The same practice is evident in the positioning of his prayer in Ephesians 1:15–20. Paul begins with a great cascade of praise, recounting the spiritual blessings that Christians have in the heavenly places, to the praise of God's glory (Eph. 1:3–14). These verses disclose the objective doctrinal realities that are the foundation of the life of the Christian and the church. Paul's next discourse will reveal the great exchange from death to life and from wrath to salvation that has taken place for all who are in Christ, by grace (Eph. 2:1–10). But again, in the middle of these magisterial disclosures of objective truth, we find the apostle praying (Eph. 1:16–23). Paul intentionally expresses dependence upon the Father to provide the subjective apprehension of all that he has revealed to be objectively true. The preacher of the gospel prays so that the people of God might "get" what he is saying about what God has done!

We see this dependence on the practice of prayer again at the conclusion of the letter. Ephesians 6:10–20 is the paradigm-shaping passage on the Christian's spiritual warfare. In this familiar passage the church is called to be strong and stand firm, buckling on the armor of the Lord. What is sometimes missed is how this standing strong in the armor of the Lord is accomplished. Verse 18 begins with the participle "praying." The placement of the participle reveals, grammatically, *how* the "stand[ing]" of verse 14 is done. The command is to stand by *praying*! In the cosmic conflict Christians *stand* on their knees.[4]

The positioning of these pastoral prayers is significant for pastoral leadership. Christ's appointed leader of his mission to the Gentiles unveils God's vision for his church: to glorify him as it grows to maturity in conformity to the image of his Son, even as it battles the opposition of Satan in this present darkness. While Paul leads toward that vision through the preaching of objective, propositional, gospel truth, he does not depend solely on proclamation of that truth. He depends *on God* to bring the understanding and experience of that truth into the lives of those to whom he preaches. At pivotal moments in the proclamation of the glorious gospel, Paul shows us how the grace and glory *objectively revealed* become *subjectively apprehended* and *practically lived* by Christ's church. Through humble, intentional, earnest dependence upon God through prayer, God's people are led forward into God's purposes from their knees.

God has blessed me with some significant mentors in my life and ministry, particularly in the practice of prayer. Victor was forty years my senior and had a habit of breaking into prayer in the middle of my conversations with him. We would be addressing a pastoral or personal issue, and he'd start praying as though the Lord was part of the conversation. When I interned with him, he would invite me into his study to kneel with him and pray if he had encountered a difficult pastoral situation. Another mentor

4   It is worth noticing, in light of our topic, that in the verses that follow (6:18–20), prayer is the instrument by which Christ's ambassador is enabled to execute the ministry of preaching the gospel.

was a seminary professor who was respected by the student body for (among many other things) his prayers. When a fellow student asked him what he remembered of our seminary's esteemed founding faculty, under whom he had studied, he said without hesitation, "their prayers!" The dependence on prayer that had been modeled for him was now being modeled by him for us. However, as profoundly formative as godly mentors in prayer are, and as thankful as we should be if God has given them to us, they all have their limits. The apostles' mentor in prayer had no flaws, failings, or limitations. They learned about the priority and pattern of prayer from Jesus.

The Messiah's Model

Luke's Gospel emphasizes prayer as a key priority in Jesus's ministry while on earth. In 5:16 we find a statement that could easily be treated in passing but is actually programmatic for Jesus's mission as Messiah: "But he would withdraw to the desolate places and pray." Luke chose to highlight this in a context where Jesus's ministry was growing in influence. Great crowds were gathering to hear him and be healed by him (5:15). Immediately prior to this, Jesus had healed a man full of leprosy (5:12–14), and immediately afterward he would heal a paralyzed man (5:17–26). It is significant that Luke makes this little statement about Jesus's habitual withdrawal to prayer in the context of his meeting massive ministry needs.

For Luke, this is a pattern in the marvelous works Christ is doing. Luke 4:40–41 shows Jesus healing, casting out demons, and preaching, when 4:42 makes a statement very similar to 5:16: "He departed and went into a desolate place." Luke 5:16 is surely illustrative of what Jesus did in that desolate place. He prayed! This is reinforced by the statement in 6:12, "In these days he went out to the mountain to pray, and all night he continued in prayer to God." In this context Christ is again fully engaged in fulfilling the mission for which he has been sent. He has healed a man with a crippled hand (6:6–10), he is about to extend his mission by appointing his apostles (6:13–16), and his practice is to withdraw for earnest prayer. Luke's emphasis comes through again in 9:18 and 28. In the context of the disciples' return from a season of intensive ministry (9:10), Jesus withdraws with them. Verses 18 and 28 show us what characterizes Jesus's times of withdrawal alone and with his disciples: *praying*. The main point of each of these narratives (and the entire Gospel) is to reveal who Christ is and what he does in fulfillment of God's redemptive promises and plan. But we would be remiss not to notice the intentional and repeated emphasis this inspired author has placed on Jesus's habit in the very midst of fulfilling that messianic mission. He repeatedly withdraws to pray.

One of the reasons this is significant for pastoral leadership is that if we are leading in imitating Christ in union with him, we ought to be conformed to Christ in his pattern of prayer. Even on Christ's mission, in the crush of leadership's opportunities and crises, we can fail to believe that prayer is actually taking action and doing something. When people and ministry needs are pressing, we can believe that the real way problems get solved and needs get met is that we work harder, talk more about the problem, or assign more material resources to it. We can think that prayer doesn't actually *do* anything. In his book *A Praying Life*, Paul Miller presented this diagnosis: "If we think we can do life on our own, we will not take prayer seriously."[5] "Self-will and prayer are both ways of getting things done. At the center of self-will is me, carving a world in my image, but at the center of prayer is God, carving me in his Son's image."[6] Christ's appointment to leadership in his cause does not render us or require us to be above desperate dependence upon God in the stewardship of the mission's needs, opportunities, and crises.

The Acts of the Apostles

After Pentecost the apostles learned to put into practice the pattern that Jesus showed them. Acts 6:1–7 is a premier case study in biblical wisdom for leadership in Christ's cause. The growing Spirit-filled church in Jerusalem had encountered an organizational problem that had become a relational problem. Exponential growth in a church without an adequate system (organizational problem) to meet the material needs of its most needy members, widows, led to the accusation (relational problem) that the Hebrew leadership of the church was prejudiced against the Hellenist members of the new community. The crisis created the risk that those who had been entrusted with the stewardship of the word (the apostles) would be distracted from their primary ministry in order to silence the false accusation and alleviate the real need. In the wisdom of God, the apostles addressed the crisis by appointing a new class of officers (Acts 6:3–6), and the apostles continued to prioritize the preaching of the word in their leadership of Christ's mission. What is sometimes overlooked is the pride of place that

5   Paul E. Miller, *A Praying Life: Connecting with God in a Distracting World* (Colorado Springs: NavPress, 2009), 59.
6   Miller, *A Praying Life*, 160–61.

was maintained for *the work of prayer* (6:4) as the apostles prioritized their leadership duties.

I recall preaching on this text when a noted biblical scholar was present. My sermon repeatedly emphasized the priorities of the word and prayer, in that order. After the sermon the scholar very graciously (as was typically his manner) approached me and simply but emphatically said, "*prayer* and the word!" I had been instinctively getting the order wrong throughout the entire sermon. The Spirit-inspired (Acts 6:4) order matters, but we can be tempted to flip the order because we emphasize the primacy of preaching. This, incidentally, is why I have placed this chapter on the practice of prayer before the one on preaching. As we shall see in the next chapter, it is right to prioritize preaching. But we can unwittingly neglect the preacher's Spirit-prescribed dependence upon God in prayer for the success of the word. The emphasis placed on prayer here discloses inseparable dual priorities for a man of God, prayer and *the word*. Prayer serves preaching and preaching follows prayer. When we neglect prayer, we subordinate (perhaps subtly) a pastoral practice that was of first importance to the apostles.

It is significant in light of this that Paul equipped Timothy for the stewardship entrusted to him this way: "*First* of all, then, I urge that supplications, prayers, intercessions, and thanksgivings be made for all people" (1 Tim. 2:1). As Paul started his instruction to Timothy on how to lead the church in Ephesus back to health, he essentially said, "*First*, pray." There might be all sorts of reasons we relegate prayer to *secondary* importance in our minds, hearts, and practice, but in the apostolic pattern for leading the church, it was of *first* importance!

John Calvin was fully aware of the risk of neglecting the relationship of prayer to the preaching of the word. He wrote:

> We shall lose all our labour bestowed upon plowing, sowing, and watering, unless the increase come from heaven. . . . Therefore, it shall not suffice to take great pains in teaching, unless we require the blessing at the hands of the Lord, that our labour may not be in vain and unfruitful. Hereby it appeareth that the exercise of prayer is not in vain commended unto the ministers of the word.[7]

Calvin is followed in this by none other than John Owen.

> I believe that no man can have any evidence in his own soul that he doth conscientiously perform any ministerial duty toward his flock, who doth not continually pray for them. Let him preach as much as he will, visit as much as he will, speak as much as he will, unless God doth keep him in a spirit of prayer in his closet and family for them, he can have no evidence that he doth perform any other ministerial duty in a due manner, or that what he doth is accepted with God. I speak to them who are wise and understand these things.[8]

The little known but immensely potent little booklet by Eugene Bradford titled *Intercessory Prayer: A Ministerial Task* points to the eight duties of the pastor that were prescribed in the Form

---

7 John Calvin, quoted in Eugene Bradford, *Intercessory Prayer: A Ministerial Task* (Boonton, NJ: Simpson, 1991), 4.

8 John Owen, quoted in Bradford, *Intercessory Prayer*, iv.

of Government adopted by the Westminster Assembly in 1645. Bradford highlights that the first of the duties mentioned is prayer:

> *First*, it belongs to his office, to pray for and with his flock as the mouth of the people unto God, Acts vi.2, 3, 4 and xx.36, where preaching and prayer are joined as several parts of the same office. The office of the elder (that is, the pastor) *is to pray* for the sick, even in private, to which a blessing is especially promised; much more therefore ought he to perform this in the public execution of his office, as a part thereof.[9]

The assembly was in step with the apostolic pattern that, for the pastor, prayer was of *first* importance.

There is another, perhaps also often neglected, dynamic to the apostolic pattern. For the apostles, prayer was not only a priority; it was also earnest and persistent. Recall how the apostles in Jerusalem described their commitment to prayer: "We will *devote* ourselves to prayer and to the ministry of the word" (Acts 6:4). The word translated "devote" means "endure in, stand perpetually ready, persevere in." It is to "be busy with, continue in, hold fast to."[10] The apostles were basically saying, "We are going to give ourselves to prayer, earnestly, busily, perpetually." This is the very thing the infant church was doing in the upper room before Pentecost (Acts 1:14), and we discover a similar picture and practice tracing the

---

9 Bradford, *Intercessory Prayer*, 1 (emphasis added).

10 See "Προσκαρτερέω," in *Exegetical Dictionary of the New Testament*, ed. Horst Robert Balz and Gerhard Schneider, vol. 3 (Grand Rapids, MI: Eerdmans, 1990), 17; and Frederick W. Danker, Walter Bauer, William F. Arndt, and F. Wilbur Gingrich, *A Greek-English Lexicon of the New Testament and Other Early Christian Literature*, 3rd ed. (Chicago: University of Chicago Press, 2000).

prayer life of the church and the apostles through the book of Acts (e.g., 2:42; 12:5; 13:1–4). In other words, when the apostles said they would *devote* themselves to prayer, they were expressing a commitment to a life of earnest, busy, persevering, protracted hard work. They were essentially saying, "This is going to be our *work*"!

In his book on revival Martyn Lloyd-Jones lamented what he referred to as "defective orthodoxy." Lloyd-Jones defended the absolute and foundational need for doctrinal orthodoxy but warned readers of "churches who are orthodox but who seem very lifeless."[11] Might one of the causes of that phenomenon be a neglect of persistence, earnestness, and laboring at prayer? Might some pastors see little of the mighty work of God because they spend too much time in organization, administration, and meetings and not enough time "lifting holy hands" (1 Tim. 2:8) to God in prayer? I will say a good deal in later chapters about the leadership practices of the preacher-leader, showing that a man of God accepts primary responsibility to lead the vision and strategy that drive the organization of the church. But many of the management activities necessary for church ministry can and must be entrusted to other leaders and members whom Christ has gifted to execute them. Too many pastors curtail the time they spend in earnest intercessory prayer in order to do the work of administration that God has gifted others to do.

Perhaps it is aspiration for organizational success, measured against cultural metrics, that lures a pastor to spend more time functioning as a CEO than leading from his knees in the "closet" and in corporate prayer. Perhaps the fear of man constrains us

---

11 Martyn Lloyd-Jones, *Revival* (Wheaton, IL: Crossway, 1987), 58.

to be governed by the expectations of those whose God-given stewardship genuinely is business administration and organization. The issue is knowing the various gifts, offices, and stewardship Christ has entrusted to us and prioritizing correspondingly. The pastor's time is his most valuable earthly resource, and he must set his priorities according to the divine prescription. How many preacher-leaders' calendars reflect a dependence upon God in earnest intercessory prayer as of first importance?

The Apostolic Prescription

This conviction concerning prayer is further reinforced when we consider that persevering prayer wasn't just the apostolic *pattern* in leading the church. It was also an apostolic *prescription* for the church. It is compelling to see some of the apostles' commands back-to-back:

> Do not be slothful in zeal, be fervent in the spirit, serve the Lord. Rejoice in hope, be patient in tribulation, be *constant in prayer*. (Rom. 12:11–12)

> *Strive together* with me in your prayers to God on my behalf. (Rom. 15:30)

> *Continue steadfastly* in prayer, being *watchful* in it. (Col. 4:2)

Notice also how Paul commends the ministry of Epaphras:

> Epaphras, who is one of you, a servant of Christ Jesus, greets you, *always struggling on your behalf in his prayers*, that you may stand mature and fully assured in all the will of God. For I bear

him witness that he has *worked hard* for you and for those in Laodicea and in Hierapolis. (Col. 4:12–13)

Finally, notice that the pattern and prescription of persevering, earnest prayer bookends the letter to Ephesus, with which we began this chapter:

I *do not cease* to give thanks for you, remembering you in my prayers. (Eph. 1:16)

. . . praying *at all times* in the Spirit, with all prayer and supplication. To that end, keep alert *with all perseverance*, making supplication for all the saints. (Eph. 6:18)

It seems clear that the kind of prayer Christ commands through his apostles, the kind of prayer that those apostles (following the pattern of Jesus) deployed in leading the church, was *not* casual, passing, perfunctory, professionalized, merely formal, half-hearted, religious custom! It was first, fervent, earnest, persevering, protracted, hardworking prayer. Bradford sums it up appropriately when he writes that, according to the scriptural testimony, when it comes to the ministers' duty, "they are to give themselves with *utter abandon* to the duty of prayer."[12]

The Apostolic Power

We cannot leave this chapter, however, under the impression that the life of the churches we lead depends ultimately on our prayers

12 Bradford, *Intercessory Prayer*, 2 (emphasis added).

or our earnestness. Returning to where we started (Eph. 3:16), we see this was not even the case for the apostle Paul. We considered the place of the Spirit and his fullness in chapter 4, "The Power for a Man of God." Now in Ephesians 3:16 we notice that the center and substance of this pivotal prayer is that the saints would be "strengthened with power" through the indwelling Spirit. This is "so that" they might know the fullness of communion with Christ (Eph. 3:17), with the final aspiration and expectation that God is able to exceed even what is prayed for, "according to the *power at work within us*" (Eph. 3:20). The apostle who assured believers that, in Christ, they have the Spirit (Rom. 8:9; 2 Cor. 1:21–22) and who commanded them to be filled with the Spirit (Eph. 5:18) bowed before the Father to strengthen them with the power of the Spirit. The leader of Christ's mission to the Gentiles depended not on his prayer or his pattern of persistence but on the person of the Godhead who powerfully effects God's will in and for believers. Earnest prayer is the means by which the man of God depends on and appropriates the power of the Holy Spirit.[13] A primary means by which God effects the indescribable, unimaginable power in the inner being of the believer and in the church is earnest, persistent prayer.

Not only is a man of God dependent on the Holy Spirit rather than his own prayer efforts, but foundational to that is his dependence upon the person and work of Christ, who patterned and prescribed prayer for his disciples. We noticed previously that Christ's example of depending on and communing with the

---

13 It is instructive how often in the book of Acts the fullness of the Spirit, along with the powerful work of the Spirit, is described in the context of *earnest* prayer (e.g., 2:1, 42; 6:4–6, 8; 8:15; 12:5, 12; 13:2–3).

Father in prayer in the midst of his mission was one of the reasons Jesus's life of prayer was significant for the life of the church and its leaders. But Christ's prayer life is recorded for us not merely, or even *primarily*, to provide a pattern to follow. First and foremost, it reveals Jesus to us as our mediator and priest, who was and even now is interceding for his people. Jesus's prayer at the conclusion of his earthly mission gives us a Spirit-inspired insight into one of the things he prayed for in those times of withdrawal. John records Jesus's prayer as he anticipated the betrayal and suffering appointed for him on behalf of his people: "I am praying for them. I am not praying for the world but for those you have given me, for they are yours" (John 17:9).

Jesus prayed for his disciples. More than that, Jesus prayed for those of us who would believe through the apostolic preaching and teaching: "I do not ask for these only, but also for those who will believe in me through their word" (John 17:20). No doubt what came from Jesus's heart and lips at the climax of his earthly mission illustrates his prayers throughout his ministry. Jesus was praying for those who would believe through the apostolic witness. He was praying for you and me!

The good news is that Christ has not stopped praying now that he is ascended to the right hand of the Father. Christ now serves as our high priest who *continually prays* for us before the Father.

> Therefore, he had to be made like his brothers in every respect, so that he might become a merciful and faithful high priest in the service of God, to make propitiation for the sins of the people. (Heb. 2:17)

We have a great high priest who has passed through the heavens, Jesus, the Son of God. . . . For we do not have a high priest who is unable to sympathize with our weaknesses, but one who in every respect has been tempted as we are, yet without sin. (Heb. 4:14–15)

Consequently, he is able to save to the uttermost those who draw near to God through him, *since he always lives to make intercession for them*. (Heb. 7:25)

When Christ ministered on earth, he delighted to be with the Father pleading for his people—pleading for *us*. He has not stopped now in heaven. Mark Jones puts this most strikingly: "There is no Christian alive who has not had Christ mention his or her name to the Father."[14] This is a gracious gospel assurance for a man of God as he stewards his work of persistent intercessory prayer. A man of God does not depend on his dutiful prayer for the life and leadership of the church on Christ's mission. He depends on Christ himself by means of the conversation with God that God himself has appointed, Christ mediates, and the Spirit empowers. In faith-fueled communion with the triune God, a man of God leads the people of God into the purposes of God, from his knees!

Conclusion

As we conclude this chapter, take time to consider your own life of prayer as a preacher-leader. Is your dependence properly placed?

14 Mark Jones, *Knowing Christ* (Edinburgh: Banner of Truth, 2015), 179. It is surely a multiplied comfort and encouragement to be assured that the Spirit also presently intercedes for God's people according to God's will (Rom. 8:26–27).

Are first things *first* in your priorities? What does your schedule communicate about where (or on whom) your dependence actually rests for the stewardship to which Christ has appointed you? There are numerous reasons leaders in Christ's church can become distracted from their duty of prayer. Fatigue, "self-medicating" through overindulgence in leisure and entertainment, struggling faith, marital discord, or unconfessed sin are a few examples. Sometimes a pastor simply has not been trained in persistent prayer. The biblical teaching reviewed in this chapter can equip us to walk in a new obedience as leaders in Christ's cause. Take time to put together a prioritized plan as to how you might give yourself with "utter abandon" to leading from your knees. Ask others to pray for you in this stewardship, as Paul did for his stewardship of the word:

> [Be] praying at all times in the Spirit, with all prayer and supplication. To that end, keep alert with all perseverance, making supplication for all the saints, *and also for me*, that words may be given to me in opening my mouth boldly to proclaim the mystery of the gospel. (Eph. 6:18–19)

> Strive together with me in your prayers to God *on my behalf.* (Rom. 15:30)

The posture of a man of God is pivotal for his leadership in Christ's cause. It is from his knees that the preacher-leader receives the power of God to be conformed to the Son of God, and to lead the people of God into the purposes of God by preaching the word of God. It is to this primary practice of pastoral leadership that we turn next.

I do not look for any other means of converting men beyond the simple preaching of the gospel and the opening of men's ears to hear it. The moment the Church of God shall despise the pulpit, God will despise her. It has been through the ministry that the Lord has always been pleased to revive and bless His Churches.

CHARLES SPURGEON

Preaching God's word is the central gift of the Spirit given by Christ to the church.

SINCLAIR FERGUSON

The Priority of a Man of God

Leading by Preaching

PREACHING IS, along with prayer, the primary task entrusted to a man of God. Men of God who have been used of God to lead his church on mission throughout history have prioritized preaching in their stewardship of pastoral ministry.

John Calvin preached an average of ten sermons every fortnight, besides several weekly lectures and other Bible studies.[1] His ministry has been accurately described as one "of unrelenting exposition of the Word of God."[2] When Archibald Alexander led

---

1 Selderhuis states that from October 1549 (the date of the city council's decision that "there should be more preaching") onward, "Calvin preached twice each Sunday and, every other week, on all workdays as well." This meant that he preached, on average, a "total of ten new sermons every fourteen days." Herman J. Selderhuis, *John Calvin: A Pilgrim's Life* (Downers Grove, IL: IVP Academic, 2009), 112. See also Nicolas Colladon, *Vie de Calvin*, quoted in T. H. L. Parker, *Calvin's Preaching* (Louisville: Westminster John Knox, 1992), 62.

2 John Calvin, *Selections from His Writings*, ed. John Dillenberger (n.p.: Scholar Press, 1975), quoted in John Piper, "Divine Majesty of the Word" (lecture, Bethlehem Conference for Pastors, February, 4, 1997).

Princeton seminary, he largely curtailed his involvement in public activities other than preaching and teaching, and when he took up his charge at the seminary, he began a Sunday evening service in his home so he could preach to the students.[3] The priority of preaching was a conviction he carried over from his pastoral ministry. Even as he argued in favor of Sunday school, an innovative approach to discipleship in his time, he emphasized the priority of preaching:

> God has indeed, appointed the preaching of the gospel as the great instrument of the instruction and moral reformation of men, and *nothing should be allowed to supersede this*; for God is wiser than man, and will moreover, honour and bless his own institutions. Let it be admitted, then, that the faithful preaching of the gospel is the *great means* to which all others should be subordinate.[4]

Men of God whom Christ has used to lead transformative movements in his mission throughout the history of the church have prioritized preaching in the stewardship Christ entrusted to them.

The principles discussed so far in this book about the leadership of a man of God find their primary application and expression

---

3 Charles Hodge, "*The Life of Archibald Alexander*, a Review," in James M. Garretson, *Pastor-Teachers of Old Princeton: Memorial Addresses for the Faculty of Princeton Theological Seminary, 1812–1921* (Edinburgh: Banner of Truth, 2012), 44. See also David B. Calhoun, *Princeton Seminary*, vol. 1, *Faith and Learning, 1812–1868* (Edinburgh: Banner of Truth, 1994), 59.

4 A. A. Alexander, "Suggestions in Vindication of Sunday Schools," in *Princeton and the Work of the Christian Ministry: A Collection of Addresses, Essays, and Articles by Faculty and Friends of Princeton Theological Seminary*, ed. James M. Garretson, 2 vols. (Carlisle, PA: Banner of Truth, 2012), 1:345 (emphasis added).

through his preaching, and the practices of leadership that take up the rest of this book all flow downstream from the pulpit. I have waited until now to address preaching directly because if preaching is to be more than a theological lecture and something entirely other than a platform for a leader's personal agenda, it is crucial to embrace the principles that are foundational to the priority of preaching. To steward preaching as the primary means of leadership God has ordained, we must know where preaching is to take the church (on its mission), who the preacher is (his appointment and character), and how he is enabled to preach as he ought (dependent on the Spirit through prayer).

But now we come directly to the compelling reason to prioritize preaching in pastoral leadership—preaching is the King's speech! It is through the preaching of his word that Christ the King himself leads his church into his purposes on his mission. The Scriptures show us the priority Christ put on preaching during his earthly ministry and now continues to do so from heaven through his servants. Following the scriptural pattern of how Christ the King executes his mission will lead us to the conviction that preaching is the priority of a man of God.

Preaching: The Priority of the King

Luke 4:16–30 tells us about the sermon Jesus preached in his home synagogue at Nazareth. Verses 17–21 record that he selected a portion of the prophet Isaiah (Isa. 61:1–2), with its promise of the Messiah, and, after reading it, announced that the promise was now fulfilled in their hearing. As we saw in chapter 1, by applying this promise to himself, Jesus announced that he was the long-awaited messianic King. This is foundational for the priority of preaching in the leadership of the church because in Luke 4:18–19 Jesus says that he will execute his mission by proclaiming. Three times in two verses it says that the Messiah's method of ministry was to proclaim![5] The Spirit-anointed King was going to bring the liberating blessings of his rule through preaching.[6] This is reinforced when Christ speaks of himself as the prophet (4:24) engaged in ministry like Elijah and Elisha (4:25–27), and Luke describes his pattern of ministry as defined by teaching with astonishing authority (4:32, 41). The chapter concludes, as we have seen, with Jesus's personal purpose statement: "I must *preach* the good news of the kingdom of God to other towns as well; for I was sent *for this purpose*" (4:43). Christ the King came to establish his rule by preaching (cf. Mark 1:15).

We could trace the priority of preaching in Jesus's ministry right through Luke's Gospel. But three high points will serve

---

5 Sidney Greidanus points out that "the New Testament uses as many as thirty-three different verbs to describe what we usually cover with the single word *preaching*. The most significant of these verbs [include] *keryssein* (to proclaim as a herald), *euangelizesthai* (to announce good news)." Sydney Greidanus, *The Modern Preacher and the Ancient Text* (Grand Rapids, MI: Eerdmans, 1988), 6. In Luke 4 Jesus identified his mode of ministry by repeatedly using *kēryssō* (4:18, 19, 44) alongside *euangelizō* (4:18, 43, 44). Luke also summarizes Jesus's ministry activity with *kēryssō* (4:44). In other words, the terms in which Jesus defined his ministry method describe, from one angle or another, *preaching*.

6 It was, of course, his substitutionary, salvific sacrifice and resurrection (along with its subsequent outpouring of the Holy Spirit) that made his rule and its blessings effective. Commenting on Jesus's preaching and healing activity during his earthly ministry, William Still writes that it was "His death and rising, which gave sanction and power to all the rest." See William Still, *The Work of the Pastor* (Fearn, Ross-Shire, UK: Christian Focus, 2001), 9. The promised blessings of Jesus's liberating rule were to be purchased and effected by the death and resurrection of the very one who was sent to preach them.

as examples. First is Jesus's assurance to John the Baptist that he is, in fact, the promised Messiah. In Luke 7:18–33 John the Baptist receives his disciples' report about "all these things" (that Jesus is doing, 7:18) and inquires through them, "Are you the one who is to come?" (7:19). Jesus's response assures John that (among other things) "the poor have good news *preached* to them" (7:22). Jesus's preaching is a distinguishing mark that should assure John he is indeed *the one* (cf. 4:18). The fact that the good news is *preached* is central to the revelation of who Jesus is. It is significant that Jesus follows this declaration with a description of John's and his own identities relative to "the kingdom of God" (7:28). John is the prophet sent to prepare the way for it (7:27), whereas Jesus is come as the Son of Man (7:34).[7] Jesus assures the greatest prophet of the Old Testament period that he, Jesus, is in fact the promised messianic King by the fact that his mission is executed primarily through *preaching* the good news.[8]

The second example is Luke's statement at the beginning of chapter 8: "He went through the cities and villages *proclaiming* and

7 As we saw with one of the biblical uses of *Son of God* (chap. 1), *Son of Man* is also a title of messianic kingship. As Begg and Ferguson point out: "Jesus is indeed both God and man. But the title 'Son of Man' means a great deal more than that Jesus was human." Alistair Begg and Sinclair B. Ferguson, *Name above All Names* (Wheaton, IL: Crossway, 2013), 101. For the biblical background of this title and its implication for the revelation of Jesus as eschatological King and the coming of God's kingdom, see Begg and Ferguson, *Name above All Names*, 101–31; and Geerhardus Vos, *The Self-Disclosure of Jesus: The Modern Debate about the Messianic Consciousness*, ed. Johannes Geerhardus Vos (Phillipsburg, NJ: P&R, 2002), 227–55.

8 See Herman Ridderbos, *The Coming of the Kingdom* (Phillipsburg, NJ: P&R, 1962), 70–76, for a discussion of Jesus's preaching of the gospel as a sign of the coming of the kingdom.

bringing the good news of the kingdom of God" (8:1; cf. 4:43). This is a summary statement of Jesus's entire ministry program. His ministry is then immediately illustrated by the parable of the sower and the seed, which points to both the Messiah's mode of ministry (spreading the word) and the place of the word in the reception of his kingdom (8:8, 10–11, 15).

The third example is Luke 9:28–36, which ties the revelation of Jesus as Messiah directly to his word. Moses and Elijah, the two greatest prophets in Israel's history prior to John (Luke 7:28), appear with Jesus at his transfiguration (9:30) as an indication of his superiority to and fulfillment of their ministries. The voice of God identifies Jesus as "my Son, my Chosen One" (9:35; cf. 3:21–22) and commands that his disciples "*listen* to him!" (9:35). Christ is revealed as the Son whose prophetic ministry supersedes Israel's greatest prophets. Not only is he the divine and Davidic king; he is also *the* man of God, and his ministry is to be received by being *heard* (cf. 2 Pet. 1:16–21). Christ the King is revealed and is to be received through his preaching![9]

---

9   The priority of preaching in Jesus's mission can also be seen from the following examples: In chap. 5 Luke turns to another revelation of Jesus's identity as messianic King, the *Son of Man*. The crowd presses in on him expressly to "hear the word of God" (5:1), and in response Jesus "sat down and taught" (5:3). Three miracles follow that reveal Jesus's authority (i.e., rule) *through his word*. First, Peter lets down his nets, explicitly in submission to his *master's word* (5:5) and catches such an extraordinary number of fish that he's compelled to respond to Jesus with homage and the confession, "Depart from me, for I am a sinful man, *O Lord*" (5:8). In the second miracle a leper is cleansed through Jesus touching him and *saying*, "I will; be clean" (5:13), which results in great crowds gathering to *hear* him and to be healed (5:15). The third of the miracles (5:17–26) leaves no doubt that their purpose is to reveal Jesus's royal identity. It is, in fact, a key event for the self-disclosure of the Messiah as he reveals himself to have *authority* as the *Son of Man*. In this episode a paralyzed man is lowered through a roof to Jesus, and Jesus pronounces the paralytic's sins forgiven (cf. 4:18).

Preaching: The Priority of the King's Servants

But the King's speech did not stop at the inauguration of his kingdom when he ascended to his throne (Acts 2:34–36; Rom. 1:4; Heb. 1:2–5). Luke's Gospel, Acts, and key New Testament passages show us that Jesus's priority during his earthly ministry continues to be how he leads the extension of his kingdom from heaven as risen King. Luke 6:12–16 records that Jesus, following a night of prayer, selected his apostles (cf. Eph. 4:11) from among the disciples. The apostles were to be his servants whom he could send to speak in his name. In Luke 9:1–2 we see Jesus giving these twelve "power and authority over all demons and to cure diseases, and he sent them out to proclaim the kingdom of God

---

The subsequent interaction with the Pharisees is calculated by Jesus to reveal that "*the Son of Man has authority* on earth to forgive sins" (5:24). *Therefore*, Jesus *says* to the man, "Rise, pick up your bed and go home." In response to this command, the former paralytic is immediately healed. In other words, in an act of intentional self-disclosure, Jesus *speaks* to express his *authority* as the *Son of Man*! Luke shows us Jesus revealing his authority and establishing his rule through his *preaching and teaching*.

Jesus's authority and the proclamation of his word are again closely related in Luke 6 and 7. In 6:1–5 Jesus's disciples pluck and eat grain from a field on the Sabbath, prompting a challenge from some of the Pharisees. Jesus rebuts their challenge by appealing to the example of Israel's premier king, David, who did the same. Jesus then asserts that his following the king's example is a disclosure of his own authority as *the Son of Man* (6:5). Having identified himself as this divine-royal figure, he once again expresses his authority primarily through his word. He does this not only by healing a man's withered hand simply by *saying*, "Stretch out your hand" (6:10), but also by delivering the "sermon on the plain" (6:20–49). After this he heals the servant of a centurion, who, as a man who understands *authority* (7:8), knows Jesus merely has to "say the word" (7:7) for his servant to be healed. "Soon afterward" (7:11) Jesus compassionately raises a widow's son from the dead, declaring, "I *say to you*, arise" (7:14), only to elicit the response from the funeral crowd, "A great *prophet* has arisen among us!" (7:16). Luke's record leads his readers to certainty that Jesus is the promised messianic King who exercised his liberating, life-giving rule *through the proclamation of his word*.

and to heal" (9:1–2); and Luke 9:6 emphasizes that his delegated authority was characterized specifically as "preaching the gospel and healing everywhere." Luke 10 makes it particularly clear that Jesus would exercise and extend his rule through his servants' preaching in his name when he says to those he has sent (now seventy-two, 10:1), "The one who *hears* you *hears* me" (10:16–17). Christ the King prepared for the continuation of his mission after his death and resurrection by selecting and sending preachers.

After his resurrection Jesus said he would extend his kingdom and authority on a global scale through the preaching of the eleven (Luke 24:47–48). He exposited the Old Testament to his disciples as the revelation of his person and work (Luke 24:25–27) and charged them to be his witnesses (24:48). His servants were to proclaim his suffering and resurrection as the fulfillment of what was written in the Scriptures (24:44, 46) and to call for the response of repentance for the blessing of forgiveness of sins (24:47). They were to make this proclamation in his name, under his authority, to all nations (24:47) in the power of the Holy Spirit, whom he would soon send (24:49; cf. Acts 1:8). The risen King commissioned his apostles to extend his rule by preaching.

Therefore, it is no surprise that after his exaltation Christ the King continues to place priority on preaching through his servants. The book of Acts, as we have seen, is the record of what Christ continued to do from heaven through his apostles. Luke's summary statements about how Christ's apostles executed their stewardship highlight the priority of preaching in their ministry. In Acts 2:42–47 we find that the church "devoted themselves to the apostles' teaching." Acts 4:32–35 tells us that "with great power the apostles were giving their testimony to the resurrection of the

Lord Jesus" so that "the word of God increased and multiplied" (12:24), "the word of the Lord was spreading throughout the whole region" (13:49), and "the word of the Lord continued to increase and prevail mightily" (19:20).[10] Preaching was the methodological priority for the servants Christ sent to continue his mission.

Preaching: The King's Speech through His Servants

The conviction that should compel a man of God to prioritize preaching is that *preaching is still the King's speech through his appointed servants!*[11] In Romans 10:14–17 the apostle Paul explains how the message entrusted to him (Rom. 10:2–13) gets out to those who need it to be saved (10:14). Having proved that the gospel he preached (i.e., Christ, revealed in the Scriptures, is God's righteousness for everyone who believes in him) is the gospel promised in the Old Testament (10:4–13), he leaves the church in the world's most strategic city in no doubt about how his mission will be most effectively executed. Paul asks "how" four times in three verses (14–17) and answers the question with this: through the preaching of those who are set apart and sent to preach the word (10:15). The astounding reason for this is revealed in verses 14 and 17. When Christ's servant preaches the word, it is Christ whom people hear (10:14), and the faith-giving word comes *from Christ* (10:17)!*[12] The conviction that drove the apostle's ministry

---

10 See Dennis E. Johnson, *The Message of Acts in the History of Redemption* (Phillipsburg, NJ: P&R, 1997), 142–49, for a discussion of these summary texts (and those related to them) as programmatic for the apostles' ministry in Acts.

11 A portion of what follows first appeared in "The Priority of Preaching in the Church's Global Mission," *Unio cum Christo* 7 no. 2 (2021).

12 See the argument made by John Murray, *The Epistle to the Romans* (Glenside, PA: Westminster Seminary Press, 2022), 386–88, esp. n16. Murray finds the argument for

methodology was that the exalted Christ still preaches through the faithful preaching of his servants (cf. Acts 26:23; 2 Cor. 3:3; 5:20; Eph. 2:7).

This apostolic conviction prompted Thomas Goodwin (reflecting on Heb. 12:25) to write, "Because he is with us ministers in delivering of [the gospel] to the end of the world; yea, Jesus Christ hath his pulpit in heaven to this day; therefore, it is said, 'Refuse not him that speaks from heaven.'"[13] John Calvin also pictured this reality most vividly for his hearers: "If our Lord gives us this blessing of his Gospel being preached to us, we have a sure and infallible marker that he is near us and procures our salvation, and that he calls us to him as if he had his mouth open and we saw him there in person."[14] Perhaps this unspoken conviction lay behind the apostles' decision to continue to prioritize the ministry of the word amid the pressing leadership needs in Jerusalem (Acts 6:2–14). Surely it affected Paul's commitment to relentless preaching in Ephesus (Acts 19:8–10; 20:20, 31) and influenced

---

the priority of preaching so strong in the text that he is careful to note: "We are not to regard the apostle as excluding or disparaging other means of communication. But this is an index of the special place accorded to the *preaching* of the gospel" (388n20).

13 Thomas Goodwin, *The Works of Thomas Goodwin*, vol. 5. *Christ the Mediator, Supereminence of Christ, Reconciliation of the People of God, etc.* (Edinburgh: James Nichol, 1863), 538.

14 John Calvin, quoted in Parker, *Calvin's Preaching*, 41–42. It is worth comparing here the Second Helvetic Confession (1566) 1.4: "Wherefore *when this Word of God is now preached in the church by preachers lawfully called, we believe that the very Word of God is proclaimed*, and received by the faithful; and that neither any other Word of God is to be invented nor is to be expected from heaven: and that now the Word itself which is preached is to be regarded, not the minister that preaches; for even if he be evil and a sinner, nevertheless the Word of God remains still true and good." See *Reformed Standards of Unity: The Historic Statements of Faith Confessed by Presbyterian and Reformed Churches*, ed. Peter A. Lillback and Bernard Aubert (Glenside, PA: Westminster Seminary Press, 2023) (emphasis added).

his choice of the final instruction he would leave with Timothy, to "preach the word" (2 Tim. 4:2).

Preaching: The Priority in Practice

So how does a man of God act when he is persuaded that preaching should be the methodological priority in the leadership Christ has entrusted to him? What difference does a conviction that Christ leads his church through his word preached make in practice? There should be at least three practical commitments that result from this conviction for a preacher-leader. He will commit to prioritizing the preached word, proliferating the preached word, and following *the* leader through the preached word.

Prioritizing the Preached Word

I began pastoral ministry during the era of the "seeker sensitive church" movement. As an expression of church growth pragmatics, the movement assessed churches (and a pastor's leadership) primarily by the number of "seekers" showing up to a church's programs, particularly its worship events. Since these events were geared to what seekers wanted, and seekers didn't want to be "preached at," churches experimented with new communication models in attempts to be relevant. I recall one church that decided to watch movies and have the pastor interpret the "narratives" to the congregation as the main event in its Sunday service rather than expositing the Scriptures. Others, in the name of being more therapeutic and practical, used popular self-help books as the text for their messages.

In our day of tweets, texts, and digital images, educators, sociologists, and psychologists discount communication methods that require attention to more than a sound bite, and they decry authoritative "lecturing," which doesn't invite the community into the "conversation." Pastors can acquiesce to this cultural philosophy or be lured to rely on tech-savvy management of media to accomplish their mission rather than committing themselves to the preparation and proclamation of the message deposited in the Scriptures. Every generation in this fallen age will seek man-made philosophies and methods to minimize and mute the heralding of God's word. Men of God in every generation must make the priority of preaching a first principle in the stewardship of the leadership Christ has entrusted to them.

This means that on principle, preaching, along with prayer, must have first priority in the pastor's personal schedule. It is worth stressing, once again, that the most valuable resource a man of God has is his time. How he spends it is the real indicator of what he believes makes the real difference in his leadership in Christ's church. A pastor faces intense pressure both within himself and from outside influences to functionally prioritize other activities that seem more opportune, effective, and measurable in terms of leadership expectations. But the preacher-leader must walk not by sight but by faith in Christ's choice of means to accomplish his purposes. He must submit his own wisdom, ideas, and agenda (as well as those of others) to the wisdom of the King and head of the church. In order to herald God's word accurately and effectively, a pastor needs to devote the best and the bulk of his time to preparation and delivery of messages from God's word. This is not the same as isolating himself in self-indulgent bookishness that neglects his people's needs and his other leadership duties. But because preaching is the primary means by which Christ the King leads his people, his ambassadors devote their time to learning and proclaiming his message. Prioritization of preaching is not just a matter of time management; it is a matter of trust in and submission to the sovereign.

Proliferating the Preached Word

If we believe that Christ speaks through his word faithfully preached, we should be zealous to multiply opportunities for God's people to hear his word preached.[15] Paul and others in church history who held this conviction were relentless in their preaching. However, most churches in North America today are being led on one thirty-minute sermon a week. Providing another worship service with another sermon is one way to proliferate the word preached.[16]

A second way is to take advantage of media God has providentially provided to spread the preached word beyond the walls of the church building. Media communication tools can be used corruptly as platforms for pastoral pride (when the goal is to build a pastor's "brand") or as weapons to harm others. But discerningly

---

15 This does not minimize the reality that God speaks to believers through the Scriptures in their own Bible reading or as believers speak the truth of the Scriptures to one another (Eph. 4:15). In fact, as we will see in chap. 10, the preaching of the word should equip believers for these very activities.

16 This seems like a reasonable conclusion even if we leave aside the discussion about whether both morning and evening worship services on Sunday are commanded in Scripture and acknowledge that the pastoral resources to share preaching duties vary based on context. Church leaders who are committed to bookending Sunday with worship services should consider investing strategic resources (see chap. 9) to support more than one pastor in order to provide preaching of comparable quality in both services and ensure that the other duties entrusted to pastors can be realistically and effectively stewarded.

stewarded digital and print media can be used locally, regionally, and beyond to carry Christ's message to a congregation's neighbors and the nations. As Christ's ambassador a pastor should develop a disciplined strategy for utilizing the tools of communication available to him in his context to propagate the word he has studied to proclaim.

A third opportunity to proliferate the preached word is to integrate it with the other word ministries throughout a congregation. A congregation's extra-pulpit ministries, such as Sunday school and small group Bible studies, can be effective venues to meet a congregation's discipleship needs, and there are good reasons why these might focus on texts and topics other than those addressed from the pulpit. But often these ministries are based on disparate curricula chosen by tradition or personal curiosity or expediency. Since the preaching of the word of God is meant to lead the people of God, the extra-pulpit ministries of a church should consider how their curriculum might intentionally move the preached word into the corners of people's lives and the complexities of discipleship.

Because the preaching of the word is the primary means by which Christ the King leads his people into his purposes, the leaders he has appointed should develop strategies (see chap. 9) to deliver his word as widely and to as many people as possible.

Following the Leader

Because preaching is the King's speech, it is imperative that what is preached is indeed the word of Christ. Leading from the pulpit does not mean a pastor imposes his personal agenda on the text of Scripture or on a congregation. It means that God's people are called and equipped to follow *the* leader as he speaks through the preached word. While this is not a book on hermeneutics or homiletics, it is essential at this point to understand what we mean by preaching that leads Christ's church.

Based on what we have seen so far, we can define preaching as God making his appeal as a man of God proclaims Christ, through the exposition of the Scripture, and through calling people to respond to him for the glory of God.[17] Preaching is not, first or foremost, about what the preacher does, the clarity of his exposition, the depth of his understanding, or the effectiveness of his communication (as important as these are). And preaching is never about the preacher's personal professional ambitions. Preaching is, first of all, the activity of God (2 Cor. 5:20; 1 Thess. 2:13)—in which the preacher is an instrument—that aims at the glory of God as its end (Rom. 1:5; 10:15; cf. Isa. 52:7; Rom. 11:36; 15:9; 16:25–27). This makes preaching the profoundly humbling and somewhat terrifying (cf. 1 Cor. 2:3) "task of tasks." The faithful preacher-leader who understands his stewardship works for the people of God to hear the plan and purposes *of God.*

---

17 Any attempt at a summary definition of this task of tasks is fraught with potential omissions. This definition seeks to emphasize, besides what we have seen already, (1) the activity of God by his Spirit; (2) the Scriptures as the final, authoritative, sufficient word of God from which the preacher draws every message; and (3) the need for response to the God who speaks. This response covers what is typically called "application" and could encompass a number of textually prescribed and contextually appropriate responses; e.g., repentance, love, and obedience, always through faith in the Christ who is revealed in and speaks through the Scripture.

The kind of preaching that most faithfully stewards this task is exposition of the Scriptures that centers on Christ. Expository preaching treats the text of Scripture as sovereign over the sermon because the God who inspired the text is the sovereign.[18] This means that "the explanation of Scripture forms the dominant feature and the organizing principle of the message."[19] The substance and structure of the sermon are determined by the particular way the portion of Scripture being preached has been delivered by the Holy Spirit.[20] This means the point of the sermon (as well as any supporting points) is exposed through accurate exegesis of the text. In other words, the agenda in the text drives the agenda of the sermon. It also means that the point of the sermon is going to be, in some way, centered on Christ. As the mediator of all revelation and redemption from God, Christ is at the center of Scripture (Luke 24:27, 44–47; John 5:39, 46; Acts 18:28; Rom. 10:5–9; 1 Pet. 1:10–12). Therefore, a sermon through which God makes his appeal will focus its explanations and applications on Christ as he is revealed in the text.[21]

---

18 I am indebted to R. Kent Hughes for this encapsulation of the sovereignty of the text as the sine qua non of expository preaching.

19 Sinclair B. Ferguson, "Exegesis," in *The Preacher and Preaching: Reviving the Art in the Twentieth Century*, ed. Samuel T. Logan Jr. (Phillipsburg, NJ: P&R, 1986), 192.

20 See Ferguson, "Exegesis," 193.

21 Timothy Keller provides this helpful description of Christ-centered exposition: "Preaching [that] grounds the message in the text so that all the sermon's points are points in the text, and it majors in the text's major ideas. It aligns the interpretation of the text with the doctrinal truths of the rest of the Bible (being sensitive to systematic theology). And it always situates the passage within the Bible's narrative, showing how Christ is the final fulfillment of the text's theme (being sensitive to biblical theology)." Timothy Keller, *Preaching: Communicating Faith in an Age of Skepticism* (New York: Viking, 2016), 32.

Christ-centered expository preaching is the kind of preaching that best equips God's people to follow their King into his purposes.[22]

The task of the preacher-leader is to be accurate about those purposes and to make their implications clear, concrete, and compelling for the contexts in which listeners live. Leading through preaching means expounding not only the doctrines deposited in the Scriptures but also the direction they set for the people who believe and follow the Christ revealed in them. It is through preaching that a man of God communicates the vision and defines the strategy God has prescribed in this word for his people to fulfill his mission. How a man of God does this is what the remaining chapters of this book are about.

Conclusion

Before we turn to how to preach the vision God has deposited in his Scriptures, take some time for some practical, personal analysis:

22 There has been reaction against certain species of Christ-centered preaching—particularly those that (1) see a redemptive-historical hermeneutic as precluding and even prohibiting application of the sermon to the life of the hearers and (2) so focus on the person of Christ that the other persons of the Trinity are neglected, if not eclipsed, in the regular preaching of the word. It should be evident by the topic of this book that I believe preaching, by its nature as God's speaking to man, must be applied (see J. I. Packer, "Why Preach?," in Logan, *The Preacher and Preaching*, 8–14). In terms of the second concern, *biblically Christ-centered* preaching will be *Trinitarian* preaching, because it is Christ who reveals the Father and Christ who has poured out the Spirit. The Father sent Christ, has spoken in Christ, and has accomplished all of his work through Christ. It is the Spirit who glorifies Christ, applies the benefits of Christ to us, and forms Christ in us. To properly center on Christ in preaching is to center on him as the mediator who reveals to us and relates us to all three persons of the Trinity. If we are preaching Christ from the text in the context of the whole counsel of God, all three persons of the Trinity should be regularly exalted and related to in concert with particular texts we are expounding.

- How do you think about preaching? Do you approach your study and the delivery of your sermons with the conviction that it is about God speaking?
- Do the time pressures of ministry cause you, functionally and emotionally, if not theologically, to relate to preaching as first about you as a preacher and your personal leadership agenda?
- What does your personal calendar reveal about what your priorities truly are? Review how your schedule really works and ask, What does this say about *what* and *whom* I trust to lead the church?
- What does the calendar of your church reveal about what is functionally primary in its leadership? Ask, Is the church I serve receiving enough of what is primary in Christ's leadership of his people?
- Can you identify some trustworthy leaders whom you could talk to and ask for prayer as you do this review? Consider asking them to help provide insight and objectivity about your personal priorities and to help provide accountability for prioritization of preaching.

The church is led into the purposes of God as a man of God, appointed by the Son of God and empowered by the Spirit of God, proclaims the word of God. If we care about stewarding Christ's mission through his church in the world, pastors must recommit themselves to the priority of preaching to accomplish God's plan and purposes. May God raise up in this next generation an army of preachers who fit the description aspired to by Charles Spurgeon:

We want again Luthers, Calvins, Bunyans, Whitefields, men fit to mark eras, whose names breathe terror in our foemen's ears. We have dire needs of such. When will they come to us? They are the gifts of Jesus Christ to the Church, and will come in due time. He has power to give us back again a golden age of preachers, a time as fertile of great divines and mighty ministers as was the Puritan age, and when the good old truth is once more preached by men whose lips are touched as with a live coal from off the altar, this shall be the instrument in the hand of the Spirit for bringing about a great and thorough revival of religion in the land.[23]

---

23 Charles Haddon Spurgeon, *C. H. Spurgeon Autobiography,* vol. 1, *The Early Years, 1834–1859* (Carlisle, PA: Banner of Truth, 1985), v.

*The power of Calvin and his fellow ministers lay
not in their talent for excoriation, but in their
ability to create a vision of a godly community.*

BRUCE GORDON

8

A Man of God Leads with Vision

Clearly Communicating Biblical Vision

"I WANT MY CHURCH to look like it did circa 1960!" This was a vision statement from a member of a church to his pastor in the foyer of their church. He had a clear picture of what his ideal church would look like. It was a picture out of the (fairly recent) past as he remembered it. "I want it to look like the good days I remember." Or consider this statement of vision: "I want us to look like the church on Spring Road. They have events every evening for people in all sorts of situations, their music is album worthy, and the pastors preach in casual clothes. They reach a lot of people who won't attend a church like ours. I want us to be like that." This person sees a need for her church to change with contemporary trends in order to meet people where they are, and she wants her church to look like other churches that appear ministry effective.

Everyone Has a Vision

People who care about their participation in church have desires for what their church would do and pictures of what it
should look like in order to achieve the mission they believe
God has given it. A person's vision might be shaped by a longing to return to an idealized past; a commitment to stay as
they are, come what may; or a compulsion to keep up with
trends for the sake of relevance. Whether or not it has been
thoughtfully developed and cleverly written out, everyone has
a vision for his or her church.

Pastoral leadership accepts responsibility in leading the
church to define and describe its vision according to the
Scriptures.

Organizational leadership scholar John Kotter defines vision
as "a picture of the future with some implicit or explicit commentary on why people should strive to create that future."[1]
The ability to capture this picture and communicate it clearly
and compellingly is a core leadership skill for any organized
community. But when the concept of developing vision is applied to pastoral leadership, it can become confused and con-
flicted. Some dismiss it as mere trendiness that distracts from
real pastoral work; others distrust it as the proverbial "camel's
nose" for corporate business culture to infiltrate the church;
and some obsess about it as though it were the "secret sauce"
for ministry success. Too often the concept of developing vision
is interpreted as a pastor's capacity to be inventive or, worse, to
impose his personal professional ambitions on the congrega-

---

1   John P. Kotter, *Leading Change* (Boston: Harvard Business Review Press, 1996), 68.

tion. But the practice of capturing and communicating vision does not need to be so complicated or risky.

For a preacher-leader, vision is captured and cast by expounding God's great purposes for his church, revealed in the Scriptures, and applying them to the particular people in the particular place and period Christ has sent him to serve. Vision is a clear picture of *what* this congregation's future could look like if God blessed his purposes *where* they live and serve (context and culture), and the compelling *why* behind the vision is the great end for all of history and redemption: the glory of God. Vision for a man of God is a picture of the future of the particular people Christ has sent him to serve as they are equipped to move forward into the purposes of God for the glory of God.

A Church's Vision Concretizes Its Mission

We have seen that Jesus's preaching was the proclamation of his word as King and that it had a clear purpose in mind—to establish and, through his apostles, extend the redeeming righteous rule of God to the hearts and lives of multitudes of disciples to the ends of the earth until the end of the age.[2] Paul represented the preaching of the apostles when he summarized his fulfillment of

2　Referring to the concept of the kingdom, Vos writes, "Not only does the conception thus stand significantly at the beginning of our Lord's work, it reappears at the culminating points of his teaching." Geerhardus Vos, *The Teaching of Jesus concerning the Kingdom of God and the Church*, ed. John H. Kerr, 2nd ed. (New York: American Tract Society, 1903), 1–2. And, "It became possible for our Lord to subsume under the notion of the kingdom the entire complex of blessing and glory which the coming order of things would involve for the people of God, and yet to keep before men's minds the thought that this new world of enjoyment was to be enjoyed as a world of God" (24).

his mission as "testifying both to Jews and to Greeks of repentance toward God and of faith in our Lord Jesus Christ," which he equated with "the gospel of the grace of God" and "proclaiming *the kingdom*" in the context of "the whole counsel of God" (Acts 20:21, 24–25, 27). This comprised the "word of his grace" that Paul saw as equipping church leaders to build up the saints toward their inheritance (Acts 20:32; cf. Eph. 4:11–13).[3] He summarized his message to the church in Corinth as the gospel "that Christ died for our sins in accordance with the Scriptures, that he was buried, that he was raised on the third day in accordance with the Scriptures" for the purpose of delivering "*the kingdom* to God the Father" (1 Cor. 15:1, 3–4, 24). We also have Luke's final summary of what the leader of the Gentile mission preached during his imprisonment in Rome: "From morning till evening he expounded to them, testifying to *the kingdom of God* and trying to convince them about Jesus both from the Law of Moses and from the Prophets" (Acts 28:23). Concluding the Acts of the Apostles, he tells us that Paul lived two years in Rome "*proclaiming the kingdom of God* and teaching *about the Lord Jesus Christ*" (28:30–31).

Richard B. Gaffin Jr. has encapsulated what these summaries tell us about the pattern and purpose of the apostle's preaching:

For any overall understanding of Paul's preaching, then, *and so for any preaching that would be faithful to his and build on it*, the following series of propositions hold:

---

3 See the exposition of Acts 20:25 in Richard B. Gaffin Jr., *In the Fullness of Time: An Introduction to the Biblical Theology of Acts and Paul* (Wheaton, IL: Crossway, 2022), 241–43.

To preach the whole counsel of God is to preach the
  kingdom of God.
To preach the whole counsel of God is to preach the
  gospel of the grace of God, with its call to repentance
  and faith.
So, to preach the gospel of the grace of God is to preach
  the kingdom of God.
Or, all together, *to preach the whole counsel of God is to
  preach the gracious gospel of the kingdom of God* by
  calling sinners to repentance and faith.[4]

To put it another way, the end purpose of apostolic mission-
extending, church-edifying preaching was the glory of God
through Jesus Christ crucified and raised, according to the Scriptures, and the accompanying implications of repentance and
forgiveness as the blessings of his kingdom.

This, in part, is why I have defined the mission of the church
as follows:

To extend the rule of God for God's glory, by proclaiming Christ
in his death and resurrection for sinners from all of Scripture, so
that multitudes of disciples are made from all nations, through
repentance and faith, who submit all of their life to the rule of
Christ and his commands (Matt. 28:18–20; Luke 24:46–48).

4 Gaffin, *In the Fullness of Time*, 243. As Herman Ridderbos put it, "Paul does nothing
  but explain the eschatological reality which in Christ's teaching is called the Kingdom."
  Herman N. Ridderbos, "The Redemptive-Historical Character of Paul's Preaching,"
  in *When the Time Had Fully Come: Studies in New Testament Theology* (Grand Rapids,
  MI: Eerdmans, 1957), 48–49.

The vision of a church should be a clear picture of what the future might look like if God blessed this mission in and through *this people*, in *this place*, in *this period*.[5] It should simply be exposing the great vision of God's kingdom and its purpose already contained in the Scripture and applying it in concrete terms to the people to whom a man of God preaches. Christ's and his apostles' preaching sought to establish and extend God's kingdom. Therefore, preacher-leaders who are committed to following the apostolic pattern can think of each text they preach as, in one way or another, serving that purpose.[6] In order to shepherd God's

5 For a description of developing a vision in light of a biblically defined mission, see Harry L. Reeder III, with David Swavely, *From Embers to a Flame: How God Can Revitalize Your Church* (Phillipsburg, NJ: P&R, 2008), 128–29.

6 Gaffin comments on preaching the whole counsel of God and what was of "central" and "peripheral" concern to the apostles: "The Acts 20 passage also shows the wholeness or largeness of the proclamation of the *gospel* for Paul. Here he goes on record against 'essential core' or common-denominator reductions of the gospel. For him, like Jesus before him, the gospel as the gospel of the kingdom is a comprehensive message, embracing the whole of life. To be sure, Paul knows, as we must know, how to distinguish between center and periphery in that gospel message with its implications and so within the whole counsel of God. We do not have to, or need not try to, say everything at once. Clearly the call to repentance and faith (20:21) for the forgiveness of sins (Luke 24:47) must always be present and prominent, as well as those matters 'of first importance' in view in 1 Corinthians 15:3–4. With that said, however, within the wholeness of the whole counsel, the periphery, because peripheral, is not thereby disposable or nonessential or unimportant, for it is *integral* to the whole in the sense that without it the center ceases to be truly central. Just as periphery, it is essential, 'peripherally essential,' we might say. Within the whole counsel of God, everything is necessary, but not equally necessary or necessary in the same way." Gaffin, *In the Fullness of Time*, 243–44. Vos also writes: "On the other hand, it cannot be denied that in many respects the idea of the kingdom acted in our Lord's thought and teaching as a *crystallizing point* around which several other elements of truth naturally gathered and grouped themselves in harmonious combination. . . . The idea of the church, where it emerges in his teaching, is a direct outgrowth of the development of his doctrine of the kingdom." Vos, *The Teaching of Jesus*, 8 (emphasis added).

people into God's purposes, pastors can apply the text as inspired to lead their hearers to embrace and extend God's rule in and through them in Christ (cf. Luke 11:1–2). In pastoral leadership, capturing and communicating vision is the practice of creating a clear and compelling picture of the future by exposing God's kingdom purposes revealed in the Scriptures and applying them concretely to a particular people in a particular place and period, so that they are equipped to move forward into the purposes of God for the glory of God.

Communicating a Clear Biblical Vision

The challenge is that many pastors are not equipped to make the great vision of God's kingdom purposes compellingly clear for their time and place. We have seen that John Calvin was one of the great preacher-leaders of one of the greatest movements in the history of the church. It might surprise some to know that one of the distinctives of Calvin's preaching was his commitment to making clear application of the texts he preached. Herman Selderhuis observes that Calvin's sermons "built bridges between the past and the present."[7] Calvin himself identifies the penchant for clear application to the life of the listener as essential to the preacher's task. In his sermon on 2 Timothy 3:16–17, he expounds on the purpose of Scripture and asserts:

> When I expound Holy Scripture, I must always make this my rule: That those who hear me may receive profit from the

---

7 Herman J. Selderhuis, *John Calvin: A Pilgrim's Life* (Downers Grove, IL: IVP Academic, 2009), 112.

teaching I put forward and be edified unto salvation. If I have not that affection, if I do not procure the edification of those who hear me, I am a sacrilege, profaning God's Word.[8]

For Calvin, the preacher could not content himself merely with the delivery of accurate data or dogma. He must desire and preach toward a goal in his hearers' lives, their edification in salvation.

Archibald Alexander would later state that a central purpose for preaching is "to excite the affections and lead to the resolutions which correspond to the nature of evangelical truth!"[9] In other words, preaching must address the heart in order to produce godly action motivated by godly affections. To do that, preaching must have a clear purpose. The preacher must understand and own where the Holy Spirit has purposed the text to go in the hearts and lives of his hearers. He must have a clear sense of how the particular text connects with the hearts and lives of the particular people he preaches to, in the place and time God has appointed for them, and he must take the sermon there.

Without clear purpose from the pulpit, many congregations are left "both individually and corporately . . . aimless and confused."[10] And since leadership abhors a vacuum, if preaching is not com-

8 John Calvin, quoted in T. H. L. Parker, *Calvin's Preaching* (Louisville: Westminster John Knox, 1992), 25.
9 A. A. Alexander, "The Free Church Pulpit," *Biblical Repertory* 21, no. 1 (1849): 87, quoted in James M. Garretson, *Princeton and Preaching* (Carlisle, PA: Banner of Truth, 2005), 95. This is what Alexander termed "experimental preaching." Quoted in Garretson, *Princeton and Preaching*, 192.
10 Jay E. Adams, *Preaching with Purpose: The Urgent Task of Homiletics* (Grand Rapids, MI: Zondervan, 1982), 1.

municating God's purpose for a congregation, other interests will fill the void and set the vision for the church. If preaching does not define and direct a church's purpose, something else will.

Jay Adams sought to remedy the problem of purposelessness by instructing preachers to find the *telos* (end point) of the text they are preaching. While he was not addressing the topic of leadership or vision in particular, Adams's emphasis on the *telos* provides a useful heuristic for communicating vision through preaching. The concept of a *telos* (in contrast to a "main point") echoes the eschatological-kingdom nature of the church's mission. Thinking in terms of the *telos* of a text can cue the preacher to conceive of his preaching portion as organically "of a piece" with God's entire redemptive revelation. Since the text serves a particular end in the unfolding of God's purposes, a man of God must study to understand the inspired end to which a particular text is to lead its hearers within God's plan and purpose and communicate that *telos* to his listeners' hearts and lives in clear and compelling terms. This is a pivotal concept for pastoral leadership that prioritizes preaching.

Because preaching is leadership, the preacher catches and communicates vision by seeing the kingdom *telos* of text after text in book after book and applying it, clearly and compellingly, to the mission of his church. It is important to emphasize, once again, that this does not mean the preacher seeks to bend a text to his leadership purpose; it means that, having done all of the exegetical and theological study necessary for accurate interpretation, he seeks to understand the Spirit's purpose and applies that inspired purpose to the hearers.[11] Leading

---

11 As Adams warned, "The thing to be avoided at all costs is to *impose* your own purposes on the passage. . . . What you must work for is to make His purposes your own." Adams, *Preaching with Purpose*, 29.

with vision means that the pastor exposits the glorious vision that the Holy Spirit has already put into the text of Scripture, and that he is purposeful in showing his listeners how God's great purposes apply to their hearts and lives, both corporately and individually. Vision, for a man of God, is a picture of the future of the particular people Christ has sent him to serve as they are equipped to move forward into the purposes of God for the glory of God.[12]

This approach to capturing and communicating vision has a few advantages for pastoral leadership that is committed to the priority of preaching:

- It preserves Christ's leadership of the congregation through his word by focusing preaching on the revealed purposes and priorities of the King, on whose behalf a man of God speaks.
- It infuses preaching with vision that lifts hearers' hearts beyond immediate and narrow focus on self-interests by connecting them with the grand narrative of God's historic and cosmic plan.
- It suggests biblically organic strategic initiatives that should be intentionally implemented by the church's leadership for the church's advance toward God's purposes (our topic in the next chapter).

---

12 This is not, necessarily, the same as having a clear "vision statement." Crafting a vision statement is a valuable exercise and, used wisely, can help facilitate better decision-making and direction setting for a church. However, having a vision statement is not the same thing as having vision. Vision statements don't lead congregations. Leaders with vision lead congregations!

Connecting Biblical Vision to God's People

The question then is how? How does a man of God clearly communicate vision by exposing and applying the kingdom *telos* of a particular text?

First, you must be deeply familiar with the Bible's story and its architecture.[13] No formula or technique can substitute for a life of loving labor in and under the pages of Scripture. Capturing and communicating biblical vision comes from a studied approach to the whole counsel of God that accurately interprets each text in its context, within the context of redemptive history and revelation.[14] The Spirit-given wisdom and competence to communicate biblical vision is not the result of a pastor's personal imagination or innovation in the service of professional ambition. It is not about "what I want my church to look like." It is the overflow of studied submission to God's own words, text after text, book after book, year of service after year of service. To put it another

---

13 For an introduction to the structure of biblical revelation, particularly as it focuses on the kingdom of God, see the works from Gaffin, Ridderbos, and Vos previously cited.

14 This is similar to the exegetically and hermeneutically informed "instinct" that Sinclair Ferguson suggests undergirds many seasoned preachers' preaching of Christ, particularly from the Old Testament. He writes: "[Perhaps most] outstanding preachers of the Bible (and of Christ in all of Scripture) are so instinctively. Ask them what their formula is and you will draw a blank expression. The principles they use have been developed unconsciously, through a combination of native ability, gift and experience as listeners and preachers. Some men might struggle to give a series of lectures on how they go about preaching. Why? Because what they have developed is an instinct; preaching biblically has become their native language. They are able to use the grammar of biblical theology, without reflecting on what part of speech they are using." Sinclair B. Ferguson, *Preaching Christ from the Old Testament: Developing a Christ Centered Instinct*, PT Media Paper 2 (London: Proclamation Trust, 2002). I suggest the same is true for understanding how a text being preached functions in the unfolding revelation of God's kingdom and its King.

way, the visionary preacher-leader is a man who has "seen" the future that God's word has prescribed for his people and who is compelled to communicate what God has shown him.

Second, you must be deeply familiar with the story and situation of the people Christ has sent you to lead. There is a symbiotic relationship between leadership and preaching in this regard. A man of God must know the people Christ has entrusted to him and their context in order to know their needs, the trends and idols of their culture, and the kingdom opportunities and obstacles in their community.[15] The kingdom concerns and possibilities he "sees" will serve as cues to the purposes of Christ's rule that should be given practical prominence as they emerge from particular texts. Clear and compelling application of the text is the fruit of knowing not only the text but also the people, the place, and the period in which God has appointed your stewardship.

Third, you must apply God's biblically revealed purposes in concrete terms for this people in this place and time. Vision is not merely the restatement of familiar theological maxims. It is the concrete connection of God's plan to *this* church, in *this* community, in *this* culture, at *this* moment, and, particularly, how it might affect their future. In order for these applications to lead the church on its mission, they must focus on the body as a whole, as well as the individual listener.

It is striking to notice how often the New Testament Epistles make application of the gospel *first* to the Christian community. The applications that we predominantly hear and listen

---

15 For inspiration and strategies to know the sheep you are leading, I recommend Timothy Z. Witmer, *The Shepherd Leader: Achieving Effective Shepherding in Your Church* (Phillipsburg, NJ: P&R, 2010), 107–37.

for in preaching—"what this has to do with *me*, *my* family, *my* work, *my* marriage"—often come *after* the body as a community is addressed.[16] This is important to keep in mind for preaching in general, but particularly for preaching that seeks to lead any systemic change in a congregation. For real change to take place, a congregation will have to move *together*, and application of the purposes and priorities of God's word should regularly appeal to the corporate body to follow Christ into his prescribed future together. This is not to suggest that the corporate is primary or exclusive, but much preaching defaults exclusively to application to the individual. This imbalance needs to be corrected if preaching envisions community-wide change.

Fourth, you must communicate the vision compellingly by addressing your hearers' hearts. Timothy Keller points out that for preaching to change people and congregations, it must capture their hearts. He writes:

Whatever captures the heart's trust and love also controls the feelings and behavior. What the heart most wants the mind finds reasonable, the emotions find valuable, and the will finds doable. . . . Your loves show what you actually believe in, not what you say you do. People, therefore, change not by merely changing their thinking but by changing what they love most. Such a shift requires nothing *less* than changing our thinking, but it entails much more.[17]

16 See, for example, the structure of Ephesians and Colossians.

17 Timothy Keller, *Preaching: Communicating Faith in an Age of Skepticism* (New York: Viking, 2016), 159. Note Keller's summary assertion that "the goal of the sermon

Biblical vision must be communicated to capture the hearts of God's people, as well as their heads. The process of pastoral leadership involves not only instructing but also inspiring God's people to move forward into God's purposes for them.[18]

This is perhaps where some biblically accurate preaching and leadership seems to misfire. Preachers address the truth to the listener's head (as they must) but not to the affections of the heart. God's people will follow the leadership of preaching that captures their hearts and their heads with a biblically compelling vision. Keller is on point when he asserts that the biblical paradigm for preaching aspires to "reshape the foundations of listeners' hearts . . . what they most fundamentally love, hope, and put their faith in."[19] Put differently, compelling preaching captures the hearer's imagination.[20]

While vision is not merely the product of the preacher-leader's imagination, clear, compelling, and concrete application does call for a prayerfully and biblically grounded imagination on the part of the preacher. A man of God will ask (based on what he has seen God's purpose to be in Scripture, what he has seen of how God has worked in church history, and what he has seen of the situation in his context), What could the implications of this text look like if God were pleased to extend his kingdom? In other words, he will try to see the

---

cannot be merely to make the truth clear and understandable to the mind, but must also be to make it gripping to the heart" (160).

18 Dwight D. Eisenhower reportedly said, "The art of leadership is making right decisions, then getting men to *want* to carry them out." Quoted in Stephen E. Ambrose, *Eisenhower: Soldier and President* (New York: Simon & Schuster, 1990), 82.

19 Keller, *Preaching*, 17.

20 Keller, *Preaching*, 21.

implications of the great texts and purposes of Scripture for this people, in this place, at this time, and in the future. He will try to imagine what it might look like if God were to bless biblically studied, historically rooted, contextually informed prayers, and he will point applications of texts there. Communicating a compelling vision requires thoughtful pastoral reflection on and kingdom aspiration for the situation of the people to whom he preaches.

Because preaching is leadership, pastors should consider not only how to make accurate, profitable, personal applications in a sermon but also how to preach in a way that clearly communicates vision. Because God's people must be led by the word of their King, vision must emerge from the text of his Scripture. If the preacher has understood the text's purpose in revealing the establishment and extension of Christ's kingdom, this vision should become clearer week after week, month after month, from the tapestry of *teloi* woven through his preaching. It is crucial that a pastor-leader makes the Scripture-driven kingdom vision concrete in the world in which his listeners live and applies it compellingly to their hearts. As Harry Reeder has put it:

> It is crucial that you set before the people a positive, clear, and concise biblical vision for the church coming back to life. . . . God's people must be called to action that is faithful to the Word of God. They must be given the kind of confidence that only the promises of God's Word can provide.[21]

---

21 Harry L. Reeder III, "Revitalizing a Dying Church," in *The Pastor-Evangelist*, ed. Roger S. Greenway (Phillipsburg, NJ: P&R, 1987), 170.

Conclusion

Preaching is the priority of a man of God. But the goal of preaching is not merely to be accurate and sound (though it is no less) but also to connect with listeners where they live so that they are led forward into God's purposes. Preaching that leads not only expounds the doctrines deposited in the Scriptures; it also communicates the direction that they set for people who believe and follow the Christ revealed in them.[22] Pastoral leadership that prioritizes preaching will communicate kingdom purposes clearly, compellingly, and concretely for the people entrusted to its stewardship.

---

22 It bears repeating that, as we develop sensitivity to the kingdom purposes of our texts and apply them to our listeners, both as a community and as individuals, we do not leave our *Christ-centered* preaching commitments. Every kingdom purpose and priority and its application to the lives of God's people must be seen *through Christ* and embraced *in Christ, by faith*! In other words, when we expose the vision-forming *telos*, we will be asking and answering, How is this the revelation of Christ the King? or How is participation in this the fruit of union with Christ? or How is obedience to this imitation of Christ? or How does what *we do* with this kingdom priority flow from the *indicative* of what Christ has already accomplished?

I do not want you to be unaware, brothers, that I have often intended to come to you (but thus far have been prevented), in order that I may reap some harvest among you as well as among the rest of the Gentiles. . . . I hope to see you in passing as I go to Spain, and to be helped on my journey there by you once I have enjoyed your company for a while. At present, however, I am going to Jerusalem bringing aid to the saints.

ROMANS 1:13; 15:24–25

I tell this story to illustrate the truth of the statement I heard long ago in the Army: Plans are worthless, but planning is everything.

DWIGHT D. EISENHOWER

9

A Man of God Leads
with Strategy

Defining and Being Dedicated to Biblical Priorities

JIM COLLINS tells the story of Roald Amundsen and Robert Falcon Scott, who led two separate expedition teams to reach the South Pole in 1911. The expeditions embarked on the same mission at the same time, in the same life-threatening environment. Amundsen's team arrived first and returned home alive. Scott arrived last, and his entire team died on the return journey.

The life-and-death difference for these two expeditions was, according to Collins, how their leaders had prepared in the years before their mission. Amundsen had lived with the Inuit people to learn their ways: their clothing, their dietary practices, and how they used dogs. "He trained himself in every conceivable situation he might encounter en route to the Pole."[1] When the expedition began in earnest, Amundsen took deliberate steps to mark his return route so that he could make clear and effective decisions in the event of an Arctic storm. Scott did none of this. He took the wrong clothes and the wrong animals and, in the effort to rush to the pole first, did not prepare his way back. It's little wonder that his whole expedition lost their lives.[2]

Intentional planning for a mission equips leaders for disciplined and effective decision-making during the mission. And when the environment becomes stormy or embattled, this can make a life-and-death difference for the people pursuing the mission together. Men of God who lead the people of God into the purposes of God serve them best when they have an intentional, biblically defined plan—a strategy—to bring them to green pastures on Christ's mission.

Every Church Has a Strategy

In discussions of pastoral leadership, however, strategy can be interpreted (by proponents and skeptics alike) as supplanting God's operating manual (the Bible) with the cunning and craft of worldly wisdom. Strategy can be relied upon to manufacture this-worldly success, or it can be distrusted as an inherently secular addition to spiritual ministry. But, as with vision, everyone has a strategy for his church. All who care about their church and have a sense of the needs, opportunities, or problems of the families and community connected to it will have opinions about what the

1   Jim Collins and Morten T. Hansen, *Great by Choice: Uncertainty, Chaos, and Luck—Why Some Thrive Despite Them All* (New York: HarperCollins, 2011), 15.
2   See Collins and Hansen, *Great by Choice*, 14–17.

priorities of their church should be, how its resources should be used, and how the pastor and leaders of the church should spend their time. One clear evidence of this is that most churches have budgets. The instant a decision-making group chooses to allot resources to one ministry over another, or to favor one program over another, they have made a *strategic* (wise or otherwise) decision.

I recall speaking with a senior leader of a very large and biblically faithful church at a conference where thousands of church leaders had come to learn from this church. When I asked him about the church's strategy, he replied rather earnestly, "Oh, we don't have a strategy!" Yet, we were at a very well-planned event at a church that had dozens of very well-planned and resourced ministries, all of which worked in concert with the pastor's highly systematic and biblically faithful pulpit ministry. And this senior leader's full-time work was to make all of this run effectively. He recoiled at the term *strategy*, but there was clearly a very intentional and (in my estimation) biblical plan to steward this church's ministry.

Or consider the well-known and rightly beloved pastor whose long-term approach to his faithful and richly blessed ministry was to have no programs for various groups in the church except the two Lord's Day services and a midweek meeting. He had, based on his convictions, intentionally defined a plan that delimited the church's priorities to a very few things. This too is a strategy. Every church has one, whether explicit or implicit, thoughtfully developed or otherwise, carefully articulated or not.

In order to steward the mission Christ has entrusted to them in the time and place he has appointed for them, leaders of Christ's church must make discerning decisions about setting priorities, use of resources, delegation of responsibilities, and more. Defining and sticking to a clearly articulated set of priorities and plan of action is not unspiritual. In fact, as we saw from Isaiah 11:1–2 (in chap. 2), it can actually be an expression of the image of God and Spirit-filled imitation of the King to whom we are united as sons and servants. Bringing order to the Spirit-empowered ministry of Christ's body images and honors the head of the church and requires intentional discernment, direction setting, and decision-making by those he has appointed to leadership. The wise King tells us that "the *plans* of the diligent lead surely to abundance" (Prov. 21:5) *and* that all of a man's plans are subject to the sovereign disposition of the Lord (Prov. 16:9). This is counsel that those who serve the King's cause must take to heart. Wisdom makes plans in submission to the sovereign will of God.

The question is not whether leaders have a strategy for their church ministry but whether their strategy is wise, identifying the right means for the right ends. For a preacher-leader, strategy is not a complex attempt to outsmart the Scriptures or to overmanage the ministry of Christ's body. Simply put, for a pastor, strategy is *the intentional definition of and disciplined dedication to biblical priorities in the ministry context Christ has appointed him to serve.* A man of God has the opportunity and responsibility to lead God's people into God's purposes by intentionally defining the biblical priorities for the church and how they can be implemented in the context of *this* people in *this* place in *this* period.

Men of God Who Had a Strategy

The leader Christ appointed on his mission to the Gentiles defined and dedicated himself to a strategy. We have seen that preaching the word was the core priority of Paul's stewardship. But the apostle also made intentional decisions about where to preach the word, where to pass by, which community should come before others, and which should serve as a center for establishing gospel work in other regions.

One example is his strategic approach to ministry to the city of Rome. Paul's epistle to the Romans contains the great doctrinal summary of the gospel he had been set apart and sent to preach. But it is also an appeal for support of his mission; the letter is bookended with statements of his plans and priorities for the execution of his stewardship (1:1–15; 15:22–33). Paul wanted the Roman believers to know that he had previously made plans to visit them in accordance with the mission he had been given (1:8–15), and his purpose in planning to visit them now was so that he could be sent on to another strategic mission field (15:22–28). All of this was in submission to God's sovereign disposition (15:32; cf. James 4:13–15).

When John Murray commented on the origin of the church at Rome, he affirmed its "strategic" position in Christ's mission and concurred with other commentators that Paul's relationship to the church of Rome resulted from his "keen eye for the strategy of a situation."[3] We have seen how John Calvin prioritized the word in the life of the church in Geneva by developing systems of pastoral care and instruction that are now commonplace in many Reformed churches. Calvin defined and dedicated himself to a strategy.

Archibald Alexander was another example of a preacher who led with intentional strategy. Recall how Alexander as a preacher's

---

3 John Murray, *The Epistle to the Romans* (Glenside, PA: Westminster Seminary Press, 2022), 13.

preacher also had a great vision for the cause of Christ in the world. But he also believed the pursuit of that vision required intentional organization beyond the pulpit. He advocated the organizing of people, establishing faithful institutions, and persuading people to become ecclesiastically connected, all the while expecting good to come from the preaching of the gospel.[4] When he pastored Pine Street Church in Philadelphia (1806–1812), the membership of the congregation "increased by more than fifty per cent" as hundreds of people were baptized.[5] He helped found institutions and societies to mobilize and multiply ministry in the city,[6] which his son, J. W. Alexander, described as "projects of his scheming and inventive mind."[7]

One example of this was Alexander's intentional advocacy for Sunday schools.[8] As mentioned earlier, Sunday school was a novel and innovative ministry in Alexander's day, and he assessed the Sunday school movement to be a "system" to which "God, in his kind providence," has directed the church's attention in order to "remedy" gaps in the church's mission to disciple all peoples.[9] Given the great need to reach people with ministry where they

---

4   See James M. Garretson, *Princeton and Preaching* (Carlisle, PA: Banner of Truth, 2005), 129.

5   David B. Calhoun, *Princeton Seminary*, vol. 1, *Faith and Learning, 1812–1868* (Edinburgh: Banner of Truth, 1994), 58.

6   Calhoun, *Princeton Seminary*, 1:57.

7   James W. Alexander, *The Life of Archibald Alexander* (Harrisonburg, VA: Sprinkle, 1991), 305.

8   See A. A. Alexander, "Suggestions in Vindication of Sunday Schools," in *Princeton and the Work of the Christian Ministry: A Collection of Addresses, Essays, and Articles by Faculty and Friends of Princeton Theological Seminary*, ed. James M. Garretson, 2 vols. (Carlisle, PA: Banner of Truth, 2012), 1:344–72.

9   Alexander, "Suggestions," 346.

are, Alexander went on to assert, "I scarcely know of a pastoral duty of higher responsibility, than to lend your utmost aid and influence to give efficiency and right direction to Sunday Schools within the limits of your parishes and vicinity."[10] Precisely as he placed the priority of ministry squarely on preaching as God's great means in accomplishing his purposes, "to which all others should be subordinate,"[11] he argued for a "system" of other extra-preaching ministries.[12] This is not to suggest that Alexander would be a friend of every program the contemporary church advocates. But in pressing pastors to wisely develop and be dedicated to ministries beyond the pulpit, and by exemplifying it, he effectively called them to lead with a strategy.

In Calvin and Alexander, not to mention Paul, we have examples of men of God committed to the priority of preaching who were also committed to defining and being dedicated to ministry strategy to carry the word to where people lived.

Defining a Biblical Strategy

How then does a pastor who is committed to the priority of preaching God's word define a strategy that equips God's people to move forward into God's purposes together? How do you steward a strategy that is so connected to what you preach that it supports the extension of the kingdom vision communicated from the word of God?

First, because preaching is leadership, *plan your preaching purposefully*. This does not necessarily mean planning a series

10 Alexander, "Suggestions," 353.
11 Alexander, "Suggestions," 345.
12 Alexander, "Suggestions," 355.

on the strategic priorities of the church, though that might be wise. It means planning your preaching through a book or series of texts far enough ahead that you are aware of the kingdom *teloi* that will regularly appear in the series, and preparing to respond to them intentionally and concretely. While you might not write the sermons in a series far in advance (many effective preachers write week to week), a preacher can "master" the message, structure, and major distinctive contributions of the book ahead of time. If you are looking for what a book of the Bible repeatedly reveals concerning God's purposes for his people (the *telos* of each text), you can be prepared to be led into strategic ministry initiatives that respond to the word.

A couple of examples might prove useful. Imagine preaching through Luke's Gospel. In your preparation, you discover that God's mercy toward the poor is a theme that will repeatedly appear in the series of expositions. You can prepare to apply that message to the congregation in concrete ways. You can initiate discussions with the church leadership about the role of deacons as leaders of ministries of mercy. You might ask: "Do we have the vision for mercy we see in the Scriptures? Do we need to reprioritize or restructure to respond rightly to the word?" The church's leadership might then begin to gather resources to equip the congregation's deacons for more mercy-oriented ministry. As the series is preached and the theme of mercy is concretely applied and the hearts of members are drawn to ministries of mercy, the leaders will be ready to respond by encouraging these ministries and providing resources to equip and enhance them. As you respond to the priorities you are seeing in the texts you preach, you can highlight these emerging ministries for this season from the pulpit. When the church drafts its next budget, ministries of mercy led by the deacons might be given significant priority in resources—not because mercy ministry is trendy or has become your congregation's "thing," but because the word preached has led the congregation to see the ministry of mercy as a strategic kingdom priority.

The same series through Luke might also lead to strategic decisions about the priority of preaching in the congregation. Because Luke-Acts repeatedly emphasizes preaching as the means by which Christ leads his church, you would regularly exposit this as the *telos* of specific texts. The church leaders could intentionally reflect on whether they prioritize the preaching of the word merely theologically and traditionally or clearly make it the functional priority in the congregation's mission. One strategic decision might be to proliferate the preached word by adding pastors to the church staff so that those called to preach will not be consumed with other needed ministries in the church. If the leadership is hearing from the texts preached that the ministry of the word is how Christ's kingdom is extended, they might also intentionally dedicate resources to getting the word out to the world beyond the walls of the church.

In these examples, the strategic decisions being made are not simply the products of church leaders gathering around a white board and dreaming of what they would like to see happen through their church. Rather, the ideas that go on the white board are responses to what Christ is saying to his church and its leadership through the exposition and concrete application of text after text from the book being preached. Having planned his preaching purposefully, the pastor is aware of the repeated themes that will emerge from accurate exposition of texts so that he can proclaim a *clear, concrete, compelling,* and *consistent* message about biblically revealed kingdom priorities. Planning your preaching to respond intentionally to the *teloi* of the texts will take the discipline of time, knowledge of your ministry context, and imagination (as to how the *teloi* of the texts concretely connect with this people in this place in this period). But this purposeful preparation can both ensure that your strategy is actually discovered from the Scriptures and equip the leaders of the church to define and dedicate themselves to ministry priorities that reflect God's purposes for his people.

Second, *define a process for church leaders to consult and collaborate with members in the trenches to discern and decide upon the ministry strategy.* While Christ's purposes and priorities for his church are discovered from Scripture, discerning how to implement those priorities in a particular congregation requires consultation and collaboration with people whose lives and ministries will be influenced by strategy decisions. Church leaders, wise counselors, and mature members of the congregation who will have insight into and legitimate interest in the consequences of decisions should have a voice in the development of the mission strategy. It is particularly important that the elders of the church embrace the wisdom of having a planned strategy for the church's mission and that they accept final responsibility for its development. This is not only because Christ has appointed a plurality of elders, including the pastor, to lead the church together. If the strategy is just "the pastor's plan," it can create a season of busy work, not real transformation in the church. Consultative and collaborative leadership is *not* the same as leading by consensus. Space does not permit a detailed description of how these two leadership models differ. Suffice it to say that in a consultative, collaborative process, those whom God has appointed to the stewardship of leadership accept responsibility, after appropriate consultation and collaboration, to make decisions even if disagreement might still exist with those who have been consulted.[13] In a consultative and collaborative process, the pastor, as the steward of God's word, has the privilege and responsibility to make biblically based recommendations to the plurality of elders and, in parity with them, uses his voice and vote as they make decisions for the direction of the church.

Planning the strategy for a church also requires the collaboration of other leaders because, unless he is particularly gifted in this area, a pastor should not be the primary manager of the planning process. He should lead the leadership to define the process (especially final decision-making responsibilities) and its participants, and he should continue to ensure that the process remains faithful to biblical mission, vision, and priorities. But he must continue to invest the best and bulk of his time

13 For a historic example of effective consultative and collaborative leadership that accepts responsibility for decision-making, see Dwight D. Eisenhower in the run-up to D-Day, in Stephen E. Ambrose, *Eisenhower: Soldier and President* (New York: Simon & Schuster, 1990), 135–40. For an accessible article on how this works in the context of organizational decision-making, see Paul Rogers and Marcia Blenko, *Who Has the D? How Clear Decision Roles Enhance Organizational Performance* (Boston: Harvard Business School Publishing, 2011), 229–48.

in his primary stewardship of preaching the word. Resources that offer assistance in this process abound, and church leaders should employ them with thoughtful biblical and theological discernment.[14]

There can also be a significant difference in the pacing necessary for the strategy-planning process of a congregation versus a privately owned business or for-profit corporation. This is a question of prudence in a pastoral context, but the need to exemplify patience and observably avoid self-will and selfish ambition with a congregation is paramount to their being able to trust the word coming from the pulpit. Shepherding sheep over unfamiliar or frightening terrain to green pastures requires willingness to be patient with the weak, so the development of a planned strategy with a church can sometimes be more protracted than with other organizations.

So, the pastor should lead church leaders to define and commit to a process that will be most faithful and effective for their particular congregation. However, any effective process will produce clear shared statements of mission and vision, defined priorities with stewardship objectives, delegation of responsibility for execution, and dedication of resources to defined priori-

---

14 For models that can be *discerningly* employed by church leaders, see particularly John P. Kotter, *Leading Change* (Boston: Harvard Business Review Press, 2012); James C. Collins and Jerry I. Porras, "Building Your Company's Vision," *Harvard Business Review,* September–October 1996, 65–77; Collins, *Good to Great: Why Some Companies Make the Leap and Others Don't* (New York: HarperCollins, 2001). For application of sound strategic planning principles to the church, see Bobb Biehl, *Master-Planning: The Complete Guide for Building a Strategic Plan for Your Business, Church, or Organization* (Nashville: Broadman & Holman, 1997); Harry L. Reeder III, with David Swavely, *From Embers to a Flame: How God Can Revitalize Your Church* (Phillipsburg, NJ: P&R, 2008).

ties. The discernment of how a particular people will devote themselves to biblical priorities in the place and time God has appointed for them should be a consultative and collaborative leadership process.

Defining Priorities

A planned mission strategy that is responsive to the preached word of God will identify the biblical priorities to which the church is compelled to devote itself. It will also help a congregation and its leadership articulate what it will *not* do.[15] A clearly defined and communicated strategy can help church leaders make more efficient decisions about the many good ideas, cultural trends, and personal projects they will be asked to endorse or embrace. A biblically responsive strategy will identify priorities like Lord's Day worship, the preaching and teaching of God's word, prayer (corporate and private), fellowship, evangelism, biblical leadership development, mercy ministries, and the stewardship of material resources, to name a few. An intentional process for defining these priorities allows church leaders not only to discern how these kinds of priorities should be implemented in their context but also to articulate their aspirations for these areas, should God be pleased to bless their stewardship. A wise steward sets objectives toward which he directs his efforts (Prov. 14:23; 21:5; 24:27; 27:23; 31:16; Luke 14:28–30), and a mission strategy should express the end toward which stewards of God's people are going to devote their God-entrusted resources.

15 See Michael E. Porter, "What Is Strategy?," in *On Strategy* (Boston: Harvard Business Review Press, 2011), 20.

The discipline of defining these stewardship objectives can be pictured with a (strategic) ministry-objective triangle (see fig. 1).

Figure 1. Ministry-objective triangle

Biblical Priority

Ministry
Objective

Congregational
Need

Resources
(Time, Talent, Treasure)

Having discerned a biblically revealed priority for the church's ministry, church leaders should assess the particular need of this people in this place in this period and also identify the resources that God has provided for this particular congregation, in terms of time, talents, and finances, to meet that need. These three factors converge to lead to the concrete expression of a ministry objective that the congregation will then dedicate themselves to pursuing *together*.

Delegating Responsibilities

A key step in stewarding the priorities identified in a mission strategy is delegating who is responsible for what and when. Many good plans fail for lack of spelling this out. A wise plan to steward the mission responsibilities and resources Christ has entrusted to church leaders should identify persons responsible for the stewardship of particular objectives and a realistic timeline for fulfilling their responsibilities. This need not, and should not, be threatening, oppressive, or punitive. But just as a man of God is accountable to have a biblically faithful sermon (or two) ready each Lord's Day and must give an account not just to those who listen but also to the Lord (Luke 12:41–43; 1 Cor. 4:1–4; 2 Tim. 2:15), likewise the faithful stewardship of other leadership responsibilities, by the pastor and others, can be encouraged by clear accountability.

Dedicating Resources

"Resource alignment is strategy."[16] Until appropriate resources have been aligned behind a stated priority, it is not a strategic priority; it is just a sentiment. Our treasure is often a more accurate indicator of our heart's commitments than what our lips profess (cf. Matt. 6:21). No matter what church leaders say their priorities are, where they choose to apportion the resources God has entrusted to them reveals their actual priorities. Just as many good plans fail because delegation of responsibility for execution is not defined in them, they also fail because appropriate resources have not been intentionally dedicated to their stated priorities. Any strategy that has a hope of impacting the mission of a congregation will reflect critical, disciplined, and sometimes courageous

16 Vijay Govindarajan, "COVID-19's Impact on the Future of Higher Education: What University Leaders Should Be Thinking about Now," Harvard Business Publishing (education webinar), June 20, 2020, https://hbsp.harvard.edu/webinars/COVID-19 -impact-on-the-future-of-higher-education/.

decisions to align resources—such as people's time and talents, and the church's shared finances—with biblically defined priorities. Until these decisions have been reached, a strategy has not been developed. To put it another way, the activities in a church that have actual resources apportioned to them (either by intention or by default) reflect its actual strategy.

The Example of Thomas Chalmers

Thomas Chalmers was one of the most influential and effective leaders in Christ's cause in the nineteenth century.[17] He has been described as "truly one of the most exemplary preachers of Christian history."[18] His renown as a preacher led to his being called to the Tron Church in Glasgow in 1815. When he arrived, the city was depressed and threatened with social upheaval, and the Church of Scotland was largely ineffective in meeting the need. The Tron parish numbered over ten thousand, but the bulk of its residents did not attend the church. Chalmers's knowledge of the Scripture and the history of the Scottish Reformation under John Knox caused him to envision a closely integrated covenant community where the parish could serve as a nucleus for the extension of the kingdom that would influence godliness throughout the nation.

---

17 Chalmers (1780–1847) exercised his most significant ministry from the beginning of his work in Glasgow (1815) until his death. The greatest impact of his pastoral leadership was felt in the Disruption that took place in the Church of Scotland, resulting in the formation of the Free Church of Scotland in 1843. For a worthwhile contemporary biography, see Sandy Finlayson, *Chief Scottish Man: The Life and Ministry of Thomas Chalmers* (Leyland, UK: Evangelical Press, 2021).

18 Hughes Oliphant Old, *The Reading and Preaching of the Scriptures in the Worship of the Christian Church*, vol. 6, *The Modern Age* (Grand Rapids, MI: Eerdmans, 2007), 633.

Chalmers began an aggressive program of pastoral visitation to gain personal knowledge of people's needs.[19] Recognizing he could not meet the needs alone, he divided the parish into manageable sections, or "proportions," providing each with an elder, a deacon, and a Sabbath and a day-school teacher. He created institutions, such as Sunday schools and day schools, along with Bible and missionary societies to support the church's mission to the parish. The strategy impacted thousands in the parish, and when he was called to another parish (St John's) in the city in 1819, he repeated and further developed this strategy.[20] The influence of Chalmers's pastoral leadership on the lives of the people of Glasgow was staggering.

When he left Glasgow to teach at St Andrews in 1823, the ministry strategy he left behind functioned fruitfully for eighteen years, enhancing the spiritual and community life of twenty thousand people. As one biographer put it, "Those who worked with him felt they were part of a magnificent mission to change the face of their parish in the name of Christ and to provide a model for the city and the nation."[21] Thomas

---

19 He personally visited each home in his parish, typically setting aside three days a week to visit, visiting seventy families a day. Consequently, in the space of one year, he visited ten thousand homes. Obviously, Chalmers did not spend much time at each home. Except in the most urgent cases, his purpose was simply to take a survey of each household and note its special needs. See John Roxborogh, *Thomas Chalmers: Enthusiast for Mission; The Christian Good of Scotland and the Rise of the Missionary Movement* (Carlisle, UK: Paternoster, 1999), 70.

20 Chalmers's approach resulted in double the number of children attending schools, from 2,370 to 4,747. The parish day schools provided children from the poorer classes with education comparable to that of children whose parents could afford private schooling. When Chalmers left St John's (his second Glasgow parish), it had four day schools, which were catering to eight hundred pupils. Roxborogh, *Thomas Chalmers*, 72, 101, 116.

21 Roxborogh, *Thomas Chalmers*, 110.

Chalmers was a man of God who intentionally defined and dedicated himself to biblical priorities in the service of the church's mission in his context. Chalmers led with a strategy.

A key to Chalmers's strategy was that he did not do it alone. Before arriving in Glasgow, Chalmers had preached a sermon expressing his conviction that the business of the ministry "is not to perform good works, but to multiply the workers."[22] He drew on that conviction to equip an army of laypeople to serve as elders, deacons, Sunday school and day school teachers, and organizers of ministry societies.[23] Chalmers's commitment to the priority of leading the saints into service enabled the word he had been sent to preach to extend beyond the pulpit into the lives in the communities where he served. It is to the practice of leading the saints into service that we will turn in our next and last chapter.

Conclusion

As stewards of the life-and-death mission of Christ's church, pastors must equip the people of God to move forward into the purposes of God through intentional definition of and disciplined dedication to biblical priorities. As they do, they must remain prayerfully prepared for God to do things they have not planned, could never accomplish, and might not choose. God is able to do

---

22 Roxborogh, *Thomas Chalmers*, 73.

23 By the end of Chalmers's ministry at St John's parish, it had twenty-five "proportions," each with an elder, a deacon, and at least one Sunday school teacher (sometimes several) and, at full strength, an agency of laymen and women that numbered close to a hundred. Each "proportion" also had a Bible society and missionary society, which were administered by the parishioners themselves. Roxborogh, *Thomas Chalmers*, 110.

more than we can ask or imagine (Eph. 3:20–21), and he does not seek, nor is he in need of, our counsel (Rom. 11:34). In the stewardship of strategy, Christ remains the sovereign, and a man of God is never more than his servant. All of our planning must be engaged with a posture of happy, humble dependence on and submission to the God into whose purposes we seek to lead his people (James 4:15).

But grace was given to each one of us
according to the measure of Christ's gift.

EPHESIANS 4:7

The gift and gifts of the Spirit serve as the external
manifestation of the triumph and enthronement of Christ.
. . . Gifts of the Spirit are given to equip the people of God
and to enable them to set on display the glory of God.

SINCLAIR FERGUSON

10

A Man of God Leads
the Saints in Service

*Developing Graces and Gifts
in Ministry on Mission*

AN ACCOMPLISHED PROFESSIONAL is asked to engage his evident abilities in a ministry that could have a transformative impact on his church and responds, with observable emotion, "I have been at this church for years, and I didn't know what my part was, until today."

A young couple are laboring faithfully to manage the care for their child with disability each Sunday, but worship and fellowship have become almost impossible. When their need becomes known, teams of members organize to serve them by taking turns caring for their child week after week. The couple is able to return to worship and benefit from the fellowship of the saints.

A small group of church members meets weekly to provide a ministry of mercy and outreach to new international residents of their community. The members are tired, feeling ineffective and under-resourced. Their pastor becomes aware of their discouragement. He provides counsel, delegates a member of the pastoral staff to provide support and training to the group, asks the deacons to allocate finances for supplies, and champions the efforts of the ministry during Sunday services. The group is reinvigorated with new direction and new workers, and some from the international community they serve begin to attend their church.

A teenager is withdrawn in his relationships and an enigma to his parents. A pastor discovers his love for music as he meets with him regularly and begins to combine teaching him the Bible with asking him to play his guitar during youth group. Through months of discipleship, the young man's faith grows and his exceptional musical abilities become evident. The pastor asks the teen to assist him by leading the singing at youth meetings, and he grows into an effective musician for the church.

These stories illustrate the sense of purpose that can fill the lives of church members and the ministry that can be multiplied in the mission of the church when a man of God devotes himself to equipping saints for service in Christ's cause.

Revisiting Ephesians 4:7–16

We have seen that Ephesians 4:7–16 is a paradigm-forming passage for connecting preaching and leadership, since it discloses a vital connection between the preaching of God's word and the extension of God's kingdom purposes in and through his people. This pivotal passage also shows us a Christ-given system, created within his body, to lead it forward on its mission as the word is preached. Christ has gifted the members of his body for service in his cause, and equipping them for that service is an end to which the preacher should lead them. God's purpose for his people is that they would not only mature in Christ but also minister for Christ. A man of God must embrace equipping the saints for service as a strategic priority if he would lead the people of God into the purposes of God.

The fundamental premise of this book is that preaching *is* leadership because Christ the King leads his church through the proclamation of his word by the servants he has sent. Ephesians 4:7–16 shows us that he does this as his servants equip the members of his body to serve. We saw in chapter 2 that the end (*telos*) of this passage is the building up of Christ's church, as his body (4:4, 12), into his *fullness* (4:13) or *image*. This is not merely a metaphor for organic growth but is the kingdom goal for which Christ has established his church. In the context of Ephesians as a whole, this growth to mature manhood (4:13) involves a realization of the new creation in Christ (1:9–10, 14; 2:10, 15; 4:24) and is tied to the new temple that is at the center of that new creation (2:19–22). In other words, the goal of growth articulated in this passage is the eschatological *telos*, within the redemptive purposes of God, that Christ established his rule to fulfill (1:9–10). The language of maturity and fullness in relation to conformity to Christ in Ephesians 4:13 ought to be heard as pointing to the renewal of that which was lost in Adam (cf. 4:24). Christ's goal for his church is nothing less than conformity to his image as *the* man! This is a primary purpose for the people whom a man of God is called to lead (cf. Rom. 8:29).

To this end, Christ the King (Eph. 4:8–10; cf. 1:20–22) has given not only preaching gifts (stewards of the word, 4:11) but also *grace* to each member of the body (4:7). Based on Paul's usage elsewhere (cf. 3:2, 7–8; Rom. 12:3–6; 1 Cor. 15:10), the grace given in this context means abilities to function in the service of building up the whole church. In light of Ephesians 4:16, this gifting is vital to the process of the body's growth and informs the purpose of the pastors listed in Ephesians 4:11. The purpose of pastor-teachers is disclosed at the end of Ephesians 4:12–13. They are "to equip the saints for the work of ministry, for building up the body of Christ" (4:12). The relationship of the phrases in this verse has been debated among faithful interpreters.[1] However,

---

1 The debate revolves around the grammatical relationship of the prepositional phrase "to equip the saints" with the phrases "for the work of ministry" and "for the building up of the body of Christ." The question is whether (in the Greek text) the two subsequent prepositional phrases grammatically correlate with or are subordinate to the first. In other words, is the purpose of the gifts in verse 11 to equip the saints *and do* the work of ministry or to equip the saints *for* the work of ministry? The view that the phrases are coordinate and that, therefore, the pastor is the one who does "the work of ministry" is reflected in the translation of the KJV, "the work of the ministry." Commentators who advocate this position include John Calvin, *Commentaries on the Epistles of Paul to the Galatians and Ephesians*, trans. William Pringle, vol. 21 of *Calvin's Commentaries* (Grand Rapids, MI: Baker, 2003), 281; Charles Hodge, *A Commentary on the Epistle to the Ephesians* (Grand Rapids, MI: Baker, 1982), 229 (though Hodge is less than dogmatic; see 230); Andrew T. Lincoln, *Ephesians*, Word Biblical Commentary (Nashville: Thomas Nelson, 1990), 253–54; and T. David Gordon, "An Equipping Ministry in Ephesians 4?," *Journal of the Evangelical Theological Society* 37, no. 1 (1994): 69–78. However, others argue that this view "faces serious syntactical and contextual difficulties" and that the last two prepositional phrases "are not syntactically parallel" but that the three prepositional phrases "build on each other." See Frank Thielman, *Ephesians*, Baker Exegetical Commentary on the New Testament (Grand Rapids, MI: Baker Academic, 2010), 278–79. For other commentators who represent this view, see Ernest Best, *Ephesians*, The International Critical Commentary on the Holy Scriptures of the Old and New Testaments (Edinburgh: T&T Clark, 1998), 398; F. F. Bruce, *The Epistles to the Colossians, to Philemon, and to the Ephesians*, The New International

since verse 12 appears in a section that begins with the disclosure that each member is gifted for service (4:7) and closes with the declaration that each member working properly is crucial to the building of the entire body (4:16), and because it is both grammatically acceptable and contextually preferable to translate the verse as the ESV does, I take the verse to mean that equipping the saints for *their* work of ministry is a key purpose for which Christ has given pastors to his church.

As we saw, this was a key emphasis in Thomas Chalmers's kingdom-expanding ministry in Glasgow. This perspective on the saints in ministry is also well represented in the Reformed pastoral tradition. R. B. Kuiper was first a professor of systematic theology and later professor of pastoral theology at Westminster Theological Seminary. In his book *The Glorious Body of Christ*, Kuiper emphasizes this crucial point:

> In the church every single member is an officer. . . . The doctrine of the universal office of believers is revealed progressively in Holy Writ. Consequently it is taught much more clearly and fully in the New Testament than in the Old. . . . In the apostolic age the universal office of believers received much emphasis. Sad to say, very soon this doctrine came to be obscured, and

Commentary on the New Testament (Grand Rapids, MI: Eerdmans, 1994), 349; William Hendriksen, *Exposition of Galatians, Ephesians, Philippians, Colossians, and Philemon*, New Testament Commentary (Grand Rapids, MI: Baker, 1978), 198; Harold W. Hoehner, *Ephesians: An Exegetical Commentary* (Grand Rapids, MI: Baker, 2002), 549; and B. F. Westcott, *Saint Paul's Epistle to the Ephesians* (Grand Rapids, MI: Eerdmans, n.d.), 63. Westcott goes as far as to say, "However foreign the idea of the spiritual ministry of all 'the saints' is to our mode of thinking it was the life of the apostolic Church" (63). That this latter interpretation is correct, in my view, is reinforced by the context of the passage, bookended as it is by 4:7 and 4:16.

after some time it was lost out of sight almost completely. . . . One of the most significant accomplishments of the Protestant Reformation was that it restored the universal office of believers to the place of honor which it deserves. . . . In the sixteenth century it became a distinctly Protestant doctrine. . . . Today there is a crying need for another revival of this doctrine. Protestantism, which once extolled it, now largely neglects it. . . . Nevertheless this office remains a reality. In every age every living member of the body of Christ is undeniably a partaker in Christ's anointing and hence a prophet, a priest and a king.[2]

John Murray, Kuiper's longtime colleague, concurs with this view when he addresses the issue of evangelism through the local church:

But although the *special office* must be given due place and esteem, this is *not the only aspect* of the church's mission. The doctrine of the *priesthood* of all believers received appropriate recognition in the churches of the Reformation. But I fear that, in our Reformed churches, the implications have been *conspicuous by their neglect* [in practice]. If there is the universal priesthood, there is also the universal *prophethood. And herein lies the mission of the church.* . . . It is this *evangelizing responsibility of the members of the church that we are so liable to neglect.* . . . No phase of evangelism *is more indispensable* to the spread of the gospel and to the building up of the church.[3]

2 R. B. Kuiper, *The Glorious Body of Christ* (Carlisle, PA: Banner of Truth, 1966), 126–31.
3 John Murray, *Collected Writings of John Murray*, vol. 1, *The Claims of Truth* (Edinburgh: Banner of Truth, 1976), 251 (emphasis added).

Sinclair Ferguson sees the outpouring of the Spirit at Pentecost as democratizing the knowledge of God and the communication of his word so that, now, all believers are "prophets as well as priests and kings."[4] When he directly addresses Ephesians 4:7–16, particularly given its use of Psalm 68, Ferguson sees the text revealing Christ as the victorious ascended King, and the functioning of the gifts he has given as "external manifestation of the triumph and enthronement of Christ."[5] The gifts Christ, by his Spirit, has given to believers are to "equip the people of God and to enable them to set on display the glory of God, the fulness of Christ, in the temple of God."[6] Ferguson goes on to explain that the gifts given for the proclamation of the word (Eph. 4:11) exercise "the dominant role in the life of the church," because it is the word that the Spirit uses to "equip the people of God to employ the specific gifts they have individually received (Eph. 4:11–16),"[7] which are "given to enable their recipients to minister to others."[8] Ferguson stresses that Ephesians 4 presents

---

4   See Sinclair B. Ferguson, *The Holy Spirit*, Contours of Christian Theology (Downers Grove, IL: InterVarsity Press, 1996), 62–63. "That which came to the people by and large through official channels in the Mosaic economy (*via* prophets, priests and kings) now belongs to all the Lord's people by Christ and through his Spirit. A status (prophet) and relationship (intimate knowledge, *cf.* Am. 3:7) with God, known at first hand only by a few under the old covenant, could now be enjoyed by all. Now all have received the messianic anointing. This is the sense in which the new covenant promise is fulfilled: 'No longer will a man teach his neighbor, or a man his brother saying "Know the Lord," because they will all know me, from the least of them to the greatest' (Je. 31:34). No longer is an anointed human mediator required to teach us to know the Lord; now all who receive the Spirit of Jesus, the exalted Prophet-Messiah, share the prophetic anointing (*cf.* 1 Jn. 2:20, 27). In Christ, they have immediate personal knowledge of God. All, in this sense, are prophets as well as priests and kings" (63).

5   Ferguson, *The Holy Spirit*, 207.

6   Ferguson, *The Holy Spirit*, 208.

7   Ferguson, *The Holy Spirit*, 208–9.

8   Ferguson, *The Holy Spirit*, 209.

a vision of each member of Christ's body as having been gifted for ministry and then equipped by those Christ has set apart to preach his word.[9]

This provides a glorious, compelling vision for the steward-ship of a man of God: the manifestation of Christ the King's glorious cosmic triumph through mobilization of his people to do ministry on his mission. Therefore, equipping the members of Christ's body for the work of ministry so that God's purpose of maturing his people in the image of his Son (4:13–16) might be achieved is a primary practice for those appointed by Christ to proclaim his word.[10] In other words, a man of God is to lead the people of God into the purpose of God *by* equipping them for ministry.

An Underemployed Ministry

However, this Christ-created system can be underemployed by preachers. Reasons for this are many. For some pastors the prob-lem may be a simple misunderstanding; the idea that saints have been gifted in order to be equipped for ministry is a new concept. Others believe that ministry is rightly done only by those holding

---

9   Ferguson seems to contrast this with a narrower view of ministry that formed in the "later church" contrary to the view of ministry presented in the New Testament teaching on gifts for ministry. He envisions that, in the New Testament church, "Manifestations for the common good (1 Cor. 12:7) in word-ministries were widespread among the people of God. Ministry in the New Testament is, in the most fundamental sense, charismatic." Ferguson, *The Holy Spirit*, 211. It is worth clarifying, however, that Fer-guson also carefully and, to my mind, convincingly makes the case for the cessation of revelatory gifts and those tied to the delivery of God's finished special revelation (223–34).

10   See J. R. W. Stott, *The Message of Ephesians* (Leicester, UK: Inter-Varsity Press, 1979), 166.

special offices in the church (i.e., the pastor, elders, and deacons). Yet others simply default to a pastor-only precedent in ministry; the culture in the church has always expected the pastor to meet all the ministry needs.

Whatever the reasons, failure to employ this Christ-given system of equipping others for ministry in a defined and disciplined (i.e., strategic) way hinders the development of needed extra-preaching ministries on the church's mission and, therefore, hinders the progress of Christ's people toward his purposes. It can also have the unanticipated consequence of relegating the goal of preaching to the mere accumulation of information by studious hearers, and not effecting the systemic transformation of the entire body that the King of the church appointed preaching to achieve. This is, in part, why I have emphasized that a strategic focus on the *priority* of the preached word should not result in the *exclusivity* of preaching. While all other ministry is downstream from the pulpit, a lot of ministry is needed downstream from the pulpit. The preaching of the word leads into other forms of ministry—that is, the ways in which members of the body minister the word to one another (Eph. 4:15; Col. 3:16), or evangelism, counseling, and so on. It is the preaching of the word that leads the saints into the ministries Christ has gifted them to do.

Employing a Christ-Given Strategy

The question is then *how*. How does a man of God develop this practice in his leadership while still prioritizing preaching? Two initial and intentional steps might be necessary: *a change of perspective* and *a change of practice*.

A Change of Perspective

Some pastors might need a reformation of their own convictions in this area. There are several reasons why a man of God might neglect or resist the strategy of leading the saints into service.

One is the *formal conviction* mentioned earlier. A pastor might actually be convinced from Scripture that only ordained stewards of the word have been entrusted with responsibility for ministry. The argument of this chapter invites a change of mind and heart on pastoral priorities in ministry. A willingness to rethink ministry convictions in submission to the Scriptures is an expression of faithful stewardship and offers hope for real transformation of both the man of God and the people he serves.

A second reason for failing to lead the saints into service might be a *functional commitment* by the pastor and the congregation he serves. While they might not hold the formal conviction mentioned above, the default *culture* of the church may be that if there is a ministry need, it is the preacher's job to fill it.

This culture might lead to a third reason for not equipping saints for ministry, *fear of change and failing others' expectations*. Leading the members of a culturally clerical church to embrace their own giftedness and call to service involves risk. Some pastors would rather remain unmanageably busy—and therefore distracted from their primary stewardship of the word in order to satisfy the expectations of congregational pollsters—than count the cost of devoting themselves to this ministry-multiplying strategy.

Fear can be the root of a fourth obstacle to a saints-equipping ministry, *fear of giving up control*. I recall discussions with pastors who lamented that members of their congregation would not accept responsibility for ministry, but close observation of these pastors' leadership showed that whenever members accepted responsibility for a ministry, the pastor would take it over or take it back. The fear that "if ministry is to be done right, I must do it myself" can be another reason a pastor might not dedicate himself to leading the saints into service.

There are perhaps other reasons that a pastor might not be committed to the strategy of equipping the saints for ministry. But if the interpretation presented here is accurate and persuasive, a man of God should intentionally work to lead his people (and himself) out of formal, informal, or fear-based resistance and to reform his pastoral theology to define equipping the saints for service as a primary, word-based strategy, and dedicate himself to it. This change of perspective should then bear fruit in a change of practice.

A Change of Practice

Given what we have seen so far in this book about the priority of preaching in pastoral ministry, as well as the functional logic of Ephesians 4:11–16, practices of equipping the saints for ministry should serve as an expression of the preacher-leader's primary stewardship, preaching the word. Because preaching is leadership, I suggest five ways for pastors to keep preaching central as they lead the saints into service.

1. *Understand that Christ-centered expository preaching equips the saints for ministry.* Equipping the saints for the service Christ has entrusted to them should not be limited to preaching a special series on this biblical strategy. As wise as that might be in certain

seasons, because Ephesians 4:12–16 demonstrates that the equip-ping of the saints is basic to a pastor-teacher's ministry, we should assume that the Christ-centered exposition of the Scriptures *will* equip the saints for their ministries. When God's people hear God's word clearly proclaimed and concretely applied to them Sunday after Sunday, month after month, year after year, they are equipped for their ministry to one another by the way their pastor divides and applies the word. When these people talk about the Scriptures with one another, they increasingly pay attention to the words of the text and how those words work in context. They become increasingly tuned to look for Old and New Testament connections that reveal the promises and their fulfillments in Christ. They develop deep convictions about the authority and sufficiency of Scripture and apply it to the ministry needs they encounter in their families, with friends, and with neighbors. Timothy Keller sees this as one of the benefits of a fervent com-mitment to exposition: "A steady diet of expository sermons also teaches your audience how to read their own Bibles, how to think through the passage and figure it out. . . . They become savvier and more sensitive readers in their own study."[11]

The pastor should regard equipping the saints for ministry not as an activity entirely distinct from his regular preaching of the

---

11 Timothy Keller, *Preaching: Communicating Faith in an Age of Skepticism* (New York: Viking, 2016), 38. Sinclair Ferguson concurs. Referring to exegetical preaching, he writes: "It teaches the congregation how to read the Bible for themselves. Most Christians tend to use in their own Bible study the style of study presented to them in the pulpit. Models of study are necessary, and exegetical preaching is the best way to teach Christians exegetical reading of Scripture." Sinclair B. Ferguson, "Exegesis," in *The Preacher and Preaching: Reviving the Art in the Twentieth Century*, ed. Samuel T. Logan Jr. (Phillipsburg, NJ: P&R, 1986), 195.

word but rather as an organic consequence of it. An intentional focus on consistently preaching the word clearly and compellingly can provide a model for the saints to follow in the exercise of their "prophethood." Intentional illustrations with ministry applications on a regular basis ("here's how this text and its truth helped me help someone") can help members see how Scripture *works* in their ministry opportunities. Preaching with theological accuracy and depth (not necessarily the same thing as being theologically technical or complex!) not only provides the saints with truth for their own worship and sanctification but also gives them foundations for their ministry to others. For many of God's people, theological maturity comes not from reading formal theological works but from what they hear Sunday after Sunday. Faithful theological interpretation and application, delivered in contextually appropriate doses, week after week, text after text, month after month can train the saints with mature, faithful theological instincts for their own ministries. As you preach the word faithfully in dependence upon the power of the Spirit with intention toward not only the maturity of God's people but also their equipping, the saints Christ has sent you to lead into his purposes will be increasingly equipped for their ministries.

2. Plan regular training sessions to extend teaching ministry beyond the pulpit. Though equipping members for ministry might not require a different set of skills than does preaching, it will require times of focused teaching that exposes church members to the biblical vision for their ministries. Keller points this out as he describes the development of Redeemer Presbyterian Church's well-known mercy ministry:

> This process starts by articulating clearly and regularly a theology of every-member ministry. . . . From the pulpit, in classes, by word of mouth, it must be communicated that every layperson is a minister, and that ministry is finding needs and meeting them with the goal of the spread of the kingdom of Christ.[12]

Planning regular *extra-pulpit* teaching can bring the Scriptures to bear at the level of tactical training to equip the saints for ministry opportunities, challenges that arise, and the abilities necessary for their specific spheres of service.[13]

3. Create intentional opportunities for conversations between church leaders and members to help members discern and steward the gifts Christ has given them. Often when a pastor embraces the role of equipping the saints, he will preach on the ministry of members, and perhaps even teach on it, but the strategy ends there. But if the ministry Christ has given each member is as important to the mission of the church as this chapter suggests, it should be as intentional a topic of pastoral conversations as other areas of their lives in Christ. I suspect this was an organic way in which ministry gifts were discerned and affirmed in the New Testament church. Given the nature of the *charismata*, it would seem appropriate to assume that service that magnified Jesus and drew others to him was affirmed by other members

---

12 Timothy Keller, *Ministries of Mercy: The Call of the Jericho Road*, 3rd ed. (Phillipsburg, NJ: P&R, 2015), 170.

13 As an example of a workable training model, see Colin Marshall and Tony Payne, *The Trellis and the Vine: The Ministry Mind-Shift That Changes Everything* (Kingsford, AU: Matthias, 2009), 69–167.

of the body (cf. Rom. 12:3–9; 1 Cor. 12–14; 1 Pet. 4:10–11). Therefore, providing opportunity for intentional conversation between members and their mature Christian friends, family, or their elders and pastors can open opportunity to discern gifts. These conversations can be woven into small group discussions, elder shepherding visits, and classes for church membership. Questions might be as simple as these:

- Do others see Jesus and say they are drawn to Jesus when you serve in the following way(s)?
- Do you experience joy and a sense of honoring God when you serve in the following way(s)?

A variety of good resources are available to assist with these intentional conversations.[14] However they facilitate them, once the leaders of a church have defined and devoted themselves to a strategy of equipping saints for ministry, they should develop a process for facilitating these kinds of conversations in their particular contexts. Make conversation about ministry giftedness and ministry opportunity an intentional aspect of your pastoral leadership strategy.

4. Align ministry resources to support members in the ministries they have been given to steward. As we saw in the previous chapter, resource alignment is strategy. Pastors and church leaders

---

14 The use of surveys of spiritual gifts, when conducted with genuine pastoral oversight and appropriate theological discernment, can also be a way to foster these conversations. Keller also suggests a list of questions that might be used in such conversations. See Keller, *Ministries of Mercy*, 173–74.

who embrace equipping the saints as a primary ministry strategy should assign a significant portion of their available resources to it if they aspire to see their ministry culture transformed in this area. If equipping saints for ministry is a biblical objective, and the congregational needs have been identified, then an appropriate allocation of the resources God has given in time, talents, and finances should be directed toward this strategy. Depending on the specific congregational context, this might include

- budgeting for training, tools, and educational materials for members;
- assigning a leader (an elder or pastoral staff member) to help members connect to ministry needs and opportunities;
- providing environments and ministry opportunities for members to discover gifts (e.g., small groups).

If appropriate resources (where God has given them into our stewardship) are not aligned with an objective, it is merely an aspiration, not a strategic priority. And, barring God's merciful supervening of unwise stewardship decisions, the objective will struggle to survive in your church.

5. *Lead members into ministry by graciously declining to take their ministry responsibilities from them.* If the pastor is apt to fill every perceived ministry gap in the church, members will not step into the opportunity or responsibility. When rightly motivated and graciously done, saying no can actually be an expression of pastoral leadership. The goal is not that the pastor can spend more time at

the gym or gaming in his basement. Equipping saints for ministry is not an excuse for negligent pastors to let God's people do what the pastor ought to be doing, or for ambitious pastors to use people as their personal tools in building their ministry kingdom. Graciously declining to usurp a saint's ministry responsibility is a response of a man of God *actively working* to equip the saints for ministry *so that* the body for which he is laying down his life can be built up.

Conclusion

As you change your perspective and practices on this Christ-designed strategy, don't expect instant or low-risk, no-fail results. A church culture where the majority of members are enjoying the ministries Christ has given them will take years, iterations, and cycles of ministry to become established. But the strategic discipline this takes is well worth the pastoral investment. Leading the saints in service is critical to the connection between preaching and leadership and the process where, for the glory of God, a man of God, appointed by the Son of God and empowered by the Spirit of God, proclaims the word of God so that the people of God are equipped to move forward into the purposes of God *together*.

Sources of Chapter Epigraphs

Introduction

William Still, *The Work of the Pastor* (Fearn, Ross-Shire, UK: Christian Focus, 2001), 17.

Chapter 1

Samuel Miller, "The Earth Filled with the Glory of the LORD," *The American National Preacher* 10, no. 7 (1835): 302 (emphasis added).

Chapter 2

John Murray, *Redemption Accomplished and Applied* (Grand Rapids, MI: Eerdmans, 1955), 161.

Chapter 4

Charles Spurgeon, *Lectures to My Students* (Grand Rapids, MI: Zondervan, 1954), 204.

Chapter 6

A. A. Alexander, "Lectures in Pastoral Theology: A Charge Delivered to J. Jones at His Ordination," quoted in James M. Garretson, *Princeton and Preaching* (Carlisle, PA: Banner of Truth, 2005), 120.

John Owen, quoted in Eugene Bradford, *Intercessory Prayer: A Ministerial Task* (Boonton, NJ: Simpson, 1991), iv.

Chapter 7

Charles Haddon Spurgeon, *C. H. Spurgeon Autobiography*, vol. 1, *The Early Years, 1834–1859* (Carlisle, PA: Banner of Truth, 1985), v.

Sinclair B. Ferguson, *The Holy Spirit*, Contours of Christian Theology (Downers Grove, IL: InterVarsity Press, 1996), 239.

Chapter 8

Bruce Gordon, *Calvin* (New Haven, CT: Yale University Press, 2009), 214.

Chapter 9

Dwight D. Eisenhower, "Remarks at the National Defense Executive Reserve Conference, November 14, 1957," in *Public Papers of Presidents: Dwight D. Eisenhower, 1957* (Washington, DC: National Archives and Records Service, 1958), 818.

Chapter 10

Sinclair B. Ferguson, *The Holy Spirit*, Contours of Christian Theology (Downers Grove, IL: InterVarsity Press, 1996), 207–8.

General Index

public and private aspects of, 32n6
stewardship of, 8
and vision, 148–49
pastoral visitation, 181
Paul
affections and aspirations of,
24–25
cross-shaped model of leadership,
97–99
farewell to church in Ephesus,
35–36
on leadership, 99, 101
prayer of, 110–12
on preaching, 135, 149, 152n6
strategic approach to ministry,
169, 171
Piper, John, 127n2
planning for mission, 166
planning preaching purposefully,
171–74
plurality of elders, 60, 174–75
practical ability, 39
pragmatic leadership, 3, 5
prayer, 80, 107–25
and power of the Holy Spirit, 122
priority over preaching, 116–18,
125
preacher
abuse of authority, 4
as herald, 52–53
needs body of Christ for care and
confrontation, 82
preaching, 127–45
as activity of God, 141
aspires to reshape hearts, 160
deprioritized, 3
exclusivity of, 193
as King's speech, 129, 133–37,
140
as leadership, 5–6

priority of, 129, 133–35, 137–39,
193
proliferation of, 139–40
teaches congregations how to
read the Bible, 196n11
priesthood of believers, 190
priorities, identification of, 177
private worship, 81
proclaiming the kingdom, 149–53
prophethood of believers, 190, 197
proportions (parish sections), 181,
182n23
Puritans, 145
purpose from the pulpit, 154–55

redemptive-historical hermeneutic,
143n22
Reeder, Harry L., III, 161
relationship, nurturing of, 81–82
resource alignment, 178, 179–80,
199–200
revival of 1857–1860, 107–8
Ridderbos, Herman, 151n4
Rubin, Eric, 48n3
ruling elders, 36n12

Samuel
leadership role of, 55–56
as man of God, 54
sanctification, 37, 76
definitive and progressive aspects,
37n16
sanctified leadership, 95–97
Scott, Robert Falcon, 165–66
Scripture
authority of, 141n17
familiarity with, 157–58
shaper and driver of ministry, xii
Second Helvetic Confession,
136n14
secret sin, 87–88

Scripture Index